BEYOND SURVIVAL

For Sybil Gottlieb
with all good wishes
17.5.82

BEYOND SURVIVAL

*Reflections on
the Future of Judaism*

Dow Marmur

Darton Longman & Todd
London

First published in 1982 by
Darton Longman & Todd Ltd
89 Lillie Road, London SW6 1UD

© 1982 Dow Marmur

ISBN 0 232 51456 9

British Library Cataloguing in Publication data

Marmur, Dow
  Beyond Survival
  1. Jewish way of life
  I. Title
  296.7′4   BM723

  ISBN 0–232–51456–9

Phototypeset by Input Typesetting Ltd., London SW19 8DR
Printed in Great Britain by The Anchor Press Ltd
and bound by Wm. Brendon & Son Ltd
both of Tiptree, Essex

To
my wife
FREDZIA
and to my children
VIVECA, *MICHAEL* and *LISA*
who taught me to believe in the future

Rabbi Moshe of Savran came to spend Shabbat in Medzebozh. After services, Reb Barukh paced up and down the room, singing 'Shalom aleikhem', welcoming the angels of peace who bring the light of Shabbat and its serenity on their wings; then he recited with his customary fervour the prayer Ribon kol haolamim – 'Thank You, Master of the Universe, for Your generous gifts – those I have received and those yet to come . . .' Suddenly he stopped and said in a loud voice: 'Why am I thanking You now for gifts to come?' He repeated the question several times, and after a long silence, began to weep.

'Why is the Rebbe crying?' wondered Rebbe Moshe of Savran. 'Because of the question?'

'Yes,' said Rebbe Barukh.

'And . . . the answer? What is the answer?' asked the disciple

'Here it is,' said Rebbe Barukh. 'We thank Him now for gifts to come – in case we will not be able to do so when we receive them'. And again he began to weep.

'Why is the Rebbe crying?' asked the disciple once more. 'Because of the answer?'

'Yes,' said Rebbe Barukh, 'because of the answer. I think of the future, which, God willing, may prove to be good to me – but what if I will be unable to give God my gratitude? How could I live without gratitude?'

Later he added: 'You see, the question is good – and so is the answer. And both make me cry.'

Elie Wiesel, Four Hasidic Masters

Contents

Preface

One deserves no blame or credit for one's parents, but one can feel grateful or hateful. It is the same with the tradition out of which one comes. What I feel is love and gratitude. If I were about to be born and could choose what people to be born into, I'd say, feeling that the wish was presumptuous and that I could not expect its fulfilment but that after all I had been asked to indicate my first choice: I should like to be a Jew.

Walter Kaufmann[1]

Many books on Judaism are written for non-Jews in the hope that Jews will read them. Because they are directed to the uninitiated, such books tend to offer a comprehensive but monolithic picture of Judaism, for their authors do not wish to trouble readers with internal divisions and endemic inconsistencies in the Jewish world. As a result, they project a false image. They create a Judaism that is of one piece, static and idyllic, without faults or blemishes. In order to offend as few people as possible, and to reach the widest possible reading public, such books almost invariably reflect a 'middle of the road' Orthodox point of view in the false belief that it approximates normative Judaism.

This book is different. It is written primarily for Jews, but in the hope that, because of this, non-Jews will want to read it too. In doing so, they will be made aware of differences in Judaism and exposed to a critique of current streams within it. The picture that should thus emerge is of a dynamic

[1] Walter Kaufmann, *Existentialism, Religion and Death* (New American Library (Meridian), New York, 1976), p. 175.

religion with clearly stated points of departure from, and points of contact with, other religions, especially Christianity.

Although the author is a Reform rabbi and a Zionist, the book is not an *apologia*, neither for Reform Judaism nor for Zionism. On the contrary, my basic conviction is that none of the existing *-isms* in contemporary Judaism meets the real needs of Jews today and, therefore, does not equip us to face the future with confidence.

Judaism has never been contained in any single movement; important aspects of it, which are authentic and significant, may be reflected in mutually opposing interpretations. It has never been *either* this *or* that; we come nearest to the essence of Judaism when we view it as the product of tensions between seeming opposites. Judaism can often be expressed paradoxically. Whenever it is being presented in terms of one stream only, ignoring or denigrating its rivals, it is being falsified. As a result, most of the popular books on Judaism do not really convey the truth, even when the facts are accurate.

The idea of tension plays an important part both in my analysis of Judaism today and in my prognosis for its future. Thus I view the *faith* of Israel in terms of the tension between God and man; the *people* of Israel as the product of the tension between the Jewish State and the Diaspora, as well as the tension between Jew and Gentile; the *land* of Israel is seen from the perspective of the tension between particularism and universalism. The future of Judaism is being considered dialectically in the firm belief that only in this way can its meaning become apparent. It is an application of Walter Kaufmann's call 'to move beyond black and white and to start thinking in colour'.[2]

This is not a handbook on Judaism, which means that it does not have much to say about past history or present observances. This is not to say that these are unimportant, but there already are competent works of that type. Instead, this book attempts to describe the kind of future that is possible for Judaism. Yet this is not a book in the genre nowadays known as futurology. It does not seek to analyze the present in order to project the future, but it does set out to identify the timeless in Judaism and suggest how this could

[2] ibid., p. 120.

be applied in the coming years and decades. In this sense it is being written as an expression of Prophetic Judaism.

In the process, therefore, what it really means to be a Jew may emerge with much greater clarity than the many attempts to define Jewish identity. Kaufmann put it succinctly: 'We have no reason to be obsessed by the question of who or what we are. The most crucial question that confronts us is what to do next.' [3] This book tries to indicate what Jewishness is by pointing to what has to be done next. As a result, it is theological, not sociological, in orientation and will be followed, it is hoped, by a systematic presentation of contemporary Jewish theology.

But there are obstacles in the way. Firstly, because it is easier to lose oneself in a discussion on identity than to commit oneself to do something, programmes of action are viewed with suspicion and scepticism, especially when they question existing assumptions. Sociology is safer than theology.

The second obstacle is more serious. To be told *what* to do presupposes agreement on *why* it should be done in the first place. Strangely, perhaps a discussion on Jewish identity does not call for a *rationale* for staying Jewish; the call to action does. A description of Judaism enables us to dodge the issue of the justification of Judaism; a response to the question what to do next does not. Debate and analysis can often shield us from personal commitment under the guise of impartiality; practical proposals make such a commitment absolutely necessary, unless the proponent is to be branded as a hypocrite. Therefore, the question of *what* to do next is linked to the question *why?* before it can address itself to the question *how?* Theology precedes not only sociology but also *Halacha*, Jewish law.

The question *why?*, which now so dominates the debate, particularly among the young, is relatively new to Judaism. The traditional Jewish question is, *how?* The fundamentals of Judaism were taken for granted like axioms or dogmas. 'The fool has said in his heart, "There is no God".' (*Psalms* 14:1). The wise man's task was to find out how to do His will. In Jewish tradition the ever-growing body of laws sought to provide the answer. That was the conventional way of stating

---

[3] ibid., p. 171.

what to do next. The contemporary way, which questions all aspects of religion, not least God, is not conducive to observances, precepts and dogmas as a way of knowing what to do. This book tries to take today's situation into account in its implicit answers to the question, 'Why stay Jewish?' In its attempt to be practical, it is theological and not *Halachic*.

We must not be satisfied with the cynical reaction, 'We have no choice'. True, even if the Jew – unlike the self-confessed 'heretic' Walter Kaufmann – would like to escape his heritage, the outside world will not let him. If we learnt nothing else from Hitler, we learnt that. But the fact that, even if the Jew wants to get away from Judaism, the anti-Semite will not let him, is only a sad comment, not a reason for staying Jewish.

I am in search of positive reasons. The negative considerations may stop us from assimilating into the surrounding culture, but only the positive ones will make us wish to affirm Judaism. The future depends on such affirmations. As a basis, I would like to put forward seven arguments in support of the claim that Jews have good reasons to stay Jewish; if their Gentile neighbours are moved by them, they, too, should be welcomed into the community, after the due process of conversion, but my primary aim is to deal with the problem: why *stay* Jewish, not why *become* Jewish.

The seven arguments are listed below as seven, almost dogmatic, affirmations. They are, however, viewed dialectically and considered in detail in the seven chapters that follow. Each reason for staying Jewish forms the basis of a chapter. Together they constitute a kind of *Menorah*, a seven-branched candlestick and ancient Jewish symbol, intended to throw some light on the future of Judaism.

The stress on the future fills me with hope that what I have written is not a mere defence of the religion of my fathers, which is the usual purpose of popular books on Judaism, but a programme for my children. The dedication suggests that I mean it personally. But, of course, I also have a wider audience in mind. As a rabbi, i.e. a teacher, of both young and old, I seek to address myself to all would-be pupils. Indeed, many of the ideas put forward here were first discussed in sermons, study groups and lectures in the congregation I serve.

Twice in the Pentateuch (*Exodus* 13:14 and *Deuteronomy* 6:20) the issue is raised, 'And when, in time to come, your son asks you, saying, "What does this mean?" ' On both occasions the answer is given in terms of the Jewish past: 'It is with a mighty hand that the Lord has brought us out of Egypt, the house of bondage.' History is, indeed, crucial to the understanding of Judaism, but it is an insufficient response to the questions that our sons and daughters ask at this time. They expect answers which also take the present and the future into account. I will attempt such answers in the seven chapters that comprise this volume. As mentioned above, each has its starting point in one of the following affirmations of Judaism.

1. *We are a link in the chain of a remarkable history*. We begin with the past. Although reference to the past is not the ultimate argument in favour of Judaism, access to our history is essential for our self-understanding. Whether observant or nonpractising, whether committed or alienated, we cannot understand ourselves unless we understand our history. By heeding the Prophet's call, 'Look to the rock you were hewn from' (*Isaiah* 51:1) we cease to be enigmas to ourselves and are able to perceive the path of our people and the purpose of our God which transcends human understanding.

2. *As Jews we understand pain, our own and that of others*. When we study Jewish history, we become aware of the suffering of our people. Through that we become conscious of the suffering of all peoples. To alleviate it becomes a religious duty, rooted in personal experience. Biography leads to ethics: 'The stranger who resides with you shall be to you as one of your citizens; you shall love him as yourself, for you were strangers in the land of Egypt: I the Lord am your God' (*Leviticus* 19:34). The very fact that we have survived points to a purpose. Significantly, the ability to remember our pain and to feel the pain of others leads to an affirmation of life, not a negation of it. It tells us what needs to be done next and this, in turn, helps us to enjoy life in spite of suffering. By contrast, those who seek to escape pain and close their eyes to the pain of others tend to lead miserable lives. To stay Jewish is, therefore, not only to know oneself better but also to enjoy oneself more.

3. *To be Jewish is to be a witness to the world*. The experience

of pain, we have said, makes us want to alleviate it in others and in so doing we come to affirm life. Our very existence, therefore, makes the world sit up and ponder upon the awesome force behind us. Staying Jewish is to testify: 'Though He slay me, yet will I trust in Him; but I will argue my ways before Him' (*Job* 13:15). By being Jews we become prophets, whether we like it or not.

4. *Judaism shows us the way to God.* Moses was told by God that 'man may not see Me and live', but that 'I will make all My goodness pass before you, and I will proclaim before you the name Lord' (*Exodus* 33:19–20). The awareness of the Jewish past, the sensitivity to pain, the act of testimony all point to God's goodness and through it His very essence can be perceived. Knowledge of Judaism leads to the knowledge of God.

5. *Judaism gives access to a unique source of wisdom.* Knowledge of our history mingled with the perception of God is the basis of Torah, which stands not only for the Pentateuch, but for the totality of Jewish teaching. Staying Jewish means having access to the distilled wisdom of a hundred generations in which God's goodness is made manifest. 'The Torah of the Lord is perfect, renewing life; the decrees of the Lord are enduring, making the simple wise; the precepts of the Lord are just, rejoicing the heart; the instruction of the Lord is lucid, restoring strength' (*Psalms* 19:8–9). The study of Jewish sources is also a source of joy and strength.

6. *As Jews we are part of a world-wide community.* Torah as a source of joy and strength manifests itself in the seemingly ordinary: in the family, in the congregation, in the community at large, in the Jewish State. The bonds we make with our fellow-Jews enable us to face the world as individuals. Social integration is in turn the basis of spiritual integration. Together they make for holiness. God manifests Himself not only through study but He also reveals Himself in the midst of the people. God is not to be found on a desert island; the whole Israelite community had to be present at Sinai. 'You stand this day, all of you, before the Lord your God . . . to enter into the covenant of the Lord your God . . . that He may establish you this day as His people and be your God.' (*Deuteronomy* 29:9–12). To be part of the community of Israel is also to have intimations of the God of Israel. Through my

fellow-Jews I am able to experience Him, even when I don't understand Him.

7. *Judaism is a source of hope.* Membership of the House of Israel is not membership of an exclusive club. The covenant between God and Israel is made 'both with those who are standing here with us this day before the Lord our God and with those who are not with us here this day.' (*Deuteronomy* 29:14). And it is the covenant, in its universal application, which is the basis of hope. God undertakes to lead us to the Promised Land, which is not only a place on the map but also the symbol of an ideal existence, provided we keep His commandments. Our actions decide our progress towards our goal. It is within our power to be the beneficiaries of God's promise. This is the realistic basis of Jewish hope and a powerful message in an age of gloom and despondency. The Jew who remains within the teachings and practices of his tradition carries the testimony of hope to his non-Jewish neighbours as 'a light of nations' (*Isaiah* 49:6) at a time of great darkness. The personal privilege of being Jewish and the public task of testimony merge: Judaism makes our lives richer and so makes it possible for us to enrich the lives of others by sharing our experience with them.

Each of the above seven assertions is the starting point of a chapter in this book. Together they seek to bring light, but not by seeking to 'sell' Judaism to reluctant Jews or to impress sceptical Gentiles. For not only the positive sides will be stressed, but also the price that has to be paid will be stated: how history can make us the prisoners of our past; how the preoccupation with pain can turn us into masochists; how testimony can become false superiority in disguise; how a God perceived in the world can be robbed of His transcendence; how the quest for Jewish wisdom can make us deaf to the wisdom of others; how the family, the community and the Jewish State can isolate us from the world; how hope can become empty utopianism. Only by looking at ourselves dialectically can we be honest with ourselves.

The future of Judaism is as endangered by those who refuse to look at its negative aspects as it is by those who fail to recognize its positive message. It is possible to be enthusiastic about the various aspects of Jewish existence and yet be critical of them, particularly in their contemporary setting. To the extent that I have been able to express both my enthusiasm and my criticism I will have made a case for a Jewish tomorrow which is neither stifled by yesterday nor misled by today.

Acknowledgements

This book would not have been written had not Lionel Blue, my friend and colleague, suggested it and had not John Todd, my publisher, encouraged me from our very first meeting. I am deeply grateful to both.

I would also like to express my gratitude to those who have helped me at each stage of writing and re-writing, especially Miss Amanda Golby, Mrs Jan Wallace and my son Michael. Rabbi Tony Bayfield read the manuscript and made helpful comments, which I greatly appreciate.

I gratefully acknowledge the copyright permission of the Jewish Publication Society of America to use their new translation of The Torah, The Prophets and The Psalms.

Transliteration has caused me considerable problems and consistency has not always been possible. For example, whereas I would transliterate the Hebrew *chet* as *ch*, some of the sources quoted use either *kh* or *h* for the same sound. Uniformity has, therefore, not been possible. I can only hope that the reader will not be unduly irritated by this.

I

THE PAST AS REFUGE

Judaism without Imprisonment

Hope implies that man is made free
from the past, as from a prison. This is
not to say that the past is forgotten, but
rather that it ceases to be the dominat-
ing factor in human behaviour.

Rubem A. Alves[1]

---

[1] Rubem A. Alves, *A Theology of Human Hope* (Anthony Clarke, Wheat-
hampstead, Herts., 1975), p. 136.

1

Jacob and Esau: The Jew after the Emancipation

The Biblical Jacob had finally settled matters with his father-in-law Laban and was now ready to continue on his journey back to Canaan. However, he was not yet out of danger, for he still had to meet his brother Esau. There was much 'unfinished business' between the two since their youth and Jacob was therefore very nervous at the prospect of the reunion, especially when he was told that Esau was on his way with four hundred men to meet him: was it to settle the old score, or to receive him 'with full military honours'? As a precaution Jacob divided his camp into two. 'If Esau comes to the one camp and attacks it, the other camp may yet escape' (*Genesis* 32:9). The wish to survive took precedence over bravery. Having made the necessary preparations and sent off his messengers, loaded with gifts and equipped with detailed instructions in tact and diplomacy (the characteristic technique of survivors), Jacob prepared himself for what might follow.

> Jacob was left alone. And a man wrestled with him until the break of dawn. When he saw that he had not prevailed against him, he wrenched Jacob's hip at its socket, so that the socket of his hip was strained as he wrestled with him. Then he said, Let me go, for dawn is breaking. But he answered, I will not let you go, unless you bless me. Said the other, What is your name? He replied, Jacob. Said he, Your name shall no longer be Jacob, but Israel, for you have striven with beings divine and human, and have prevailed. (*Genesis* 32:25–9)

Who was the mysterious being that wrestled with Jacob? One of the many answers is given by the medieval Jewish commentator, Rashi. Basing himself on ancient Rabbinic tradition, he identifies the wrestler as the guardian angel of Esau. When we bear in mind that the figure of Jacob often represents in Rabbinic literature the Jew and Esau stands for the Gentile, the significance of Rashi's interpretation becomes apparent: the Jew, epitomising the spirit of Hebraism, must wrestle with the spirit of the Gentile world in order to continue on his journey. If the latter prevails, the Jew and his tradition cease to exist. But if the guardian angel of Esau does not defeat Jacob, a blessing can be extracted – despite the pain – and Israel comes into being. Jewish existence is thus the result not of cowardice, but of extreme courage: 'Your name shall no longer be Jacob, but Israel, for you have striven with beings divine and human, and have prevailed.'

This is not an attempt at Biblical exegesis, but a pointer to the paradigm for the course of Jewish history. Since the days of 'Abram the Hebrew' (*Genesis* 14:13), Jacob's grandfather, Hebraism has had to encounter outside forces, most of the time in the Diaspora. Such encounters have always been fraught with innumerable dangers and not infrequently ended in disaster. But they have also brought great promise, the opportunity for a creative synthesis, the blessing that gave birth to Israel. In this way the continuous exposure of Judaism to the Gentile world – be it pagan, Christian or Muslim – has not only brought with it pain but also revival and hope. Wrestling in the night enabled Jacob to overcome the past and face his brother in the here and now, with confidence and love: 'Esau ran to greet him. He embraced him and, falling on his neck, he kissed him; and they wept' (*Genesis* 33:4). Jewish history is a record of the pain and the reunion, the dangers and the opportunities.

The period inaugurated by the Enlightenment and the French Revolution, which we Jews know as the epoch of Emancipation, reflects the pain and the triumph with particular poignancy. When the walls of the medieval Jewish ghetto were finally broken down, in some places as early as at the end of the eighteenth century, in others as late as the beginning of the twentieth century, Jacob once again had to wrestle with the guardian angel of Esau. During the long period of isolation in the ghetto, Judaism had in many respects stagnated. At the same time the cultural life of Europe had been developing in a spectacular manner. The Emancipation now

forced Jews and Judaism to come to terms with the new
Europe – and soon with the New World – by wrestling with
its spirit, the spirit of the Renaissance and the Reformation,
Descartes and Newton, Shakespeare and Goethe, Montes-
quieu and Jefferson.

Jews responded in many different ways. One way was to
ignore the challenge altogether and to refuse to acknowledge
the fact that the ghetto was no more, that Emancipation had
come. As the outer walls were falling, efforts were being made
by some to fortify the walls from within, thus eliminating the
reason for accepting the challenge, and the lure, of Western
culture. That is how extreme Jewish Orthodoxy has maintained itself to this day. It consistently and totally refuses to
recognize not just the validity, but even the reality, of the
modern world. Some of its exponents even continue to dress
like eighteenth-century Polish peasants in their Sunday best,
not because the garb is religiously significant, but because it
defies fashion and modernity. Other characteristic features of
their religious life are often determined by similar criteria.
This reactionary stance has of late gained new adherents not
only among Jews in the State of Israel but also in the Islamic
world, and there are signs that even the Church may be more
open to it. The failure of the West – apparent or real – has,
of course, given greater credibility and authority to all those
who refused to embrace it in the first place.

A second way of responding to the challenge of modernity
and Emancipation was total assimilation. There were many
Jews – more in the past but many still today – who avoided
the struggle with the spirit of the West even before the fight
started. They were so intoxicated by Western culture that
they happily abandoned their Jewish history and religious
heritage for the sake of integration. In addition, throughout
the nineteenth century such assimilation, accompanied by
formal conversion to Christianity, was the only way to gain
professional promotion and social acceptance. This was more
true on the Continent of Europe than in Britain, but even
England would not have had a 'Jewish' Prime Minister, Disraeli, had not his father arranged for his baptism in his youth.
Baptism became for many Jews in the post-Emancipation
period the passport to Western society. In the words of one
Jew, he converted out of conviction: he was convinced that

it was better to be a professor in St Petersburg than a school master in a Russian village. Many such converts gained a prominent place in history: Heinrich Heine, Felix Mendelssohn, Karl Marx, Benjamin Disraeli and a host of others.

The ultra-Orthodox and the assimilationists, diametrically opposed though they are, have this in common that they both have refused to accept the challenge of becoming Israel by enabling Jacob to wrestle with the guardian angel of Esau. But there were those who were prepared to wrestle, as their ancestor Jacob had done, in search of a synthesis and for the sake of authenticity. The earliest attempt was made by Reform Judaism. Later other movements came into being, notably neo-Orthodoxy and Zionism. Different though these three branches of modern Judaism may be, they all rejected the ultra-Orthodox stance and vehemently repudiated the kind of assimilationism that gives up Judaism for the sake of expediency. Together they reflected a third Jewish response to modernity, but each – Reform, neo-Orthodoxy and Zionism – had its own distinct characteristics.

Reform began in the early years of the nineteenth century in Germany and grew – notably in the United States – out of the conviction that the Emancipation heralded a new Messianic era, the fulfilment of the prophecy that now, in the Age of Reason and Tolerance, 'nation shall not take up sword against nation; they shall never again know war' (*Isaiah* 2:4; *Micah* 4:3). Therefore, for them the creative synthesis between Hebraism and Western culture meant that only the universalist aspects of Judaism were to be stressed. Any form of observance that sought to separate the Jew from his Gentile neighbour had to be carefully reconsidered and every particularist teaching modified or eliminated. Observance could not be regarded as true 'religion'; at best it was only custom and ceremonial. The Reform stance was based on the non-fundamentalist view of Revelation. The traditional, fundamentalist position is that Moses received the Pentateuch, together with the body of the so-called Oral Tradition, from God on Mount Sinai. Therefore, according to this view, both are immutable. On the basis of modern Biblical scholarship and common sense – both highly exalted by the Enlightenment – Reform found it relatively easy to refute the traditional view and to validate its own liberal position.

By and large, Conservative Judaism, which came into being in the United States at the beginning of this century, shares the liberal platform on the question of Revelation, although its emphasis may be less radical and its attitude to observance more traditional. That is why it is almost invariably included under the rubric 'Reform' in this book. Neo-Orthodoxy by contrast, offers a very different creative synthesis. If Reform and Conservative Judaism can be said to have attempted a *fusion* between Hebraism and Western culture, neo-Ortho-doxy tried to develop a form of *co-existence*. Its motto was: *Torah im derech erets*, i.e. the fundamentalist view of Scripture and Oral Tradition, combined with 'the way of the world'. Its intention was to affirm Western culture where it did not challenge or interfere with traditional Judaism. It was pre-pared to accommodate itself to 'the way of the world' only if it was satisfied that the body of Jewish law, as laid down in the medieval codes, notably in Joseph Karo's *Shulchan Aruch*, was not being altered, but only interpreted. In this its en-deavour it was severely criticized by Reform for being too particularist and bitterly attacked by ultra-Orthodoxy for being too assimilationist.

Both the Reform method of fusion and the neo-Orthodox form of co-existence are Jewish *religious* responses to the chal-lenge of Emancipation. However, the period of Emancipation was also characterized by a marked decline in religious belief and religious commitment. Since it is possible to be Jewish without being religious – for Judaism is both peoplehood and religion, civilization and belief – how was the non-believing Jew, who did not wish to assimilate, to wrestle with the guardian angel of Esau? Behind the answer to this question we find the origin of the third modernist movement in Juda-ism: Zionism, which had its origin in the last decade of the nineteenth century. Despite its firm religious roots and many religious adherents, modern Zionism is primarily a secularist movement. Although it never succeeded in becoming wholly secular – for Judaism by its very nature knows no formal distinction between religious and secular – its opponents, notably ultra-Orthodoxy and Reform, regarded it as such and opposed it for that reason. Zionism was a way for the non-religious Jew to meet the challenge of modernism and yet stay

Jewish by expressing his Jewishness in the nationalist terms fashionable since the end of the last century.

If Reform was *fusion* and neo-Orthodoxy *co-existence*, Zionism was *imitation*. It saw Jewish existence being fashioned on the same basis as the existence of any other people. Its motto was, 'We are a nation like any other nation'. Hebrew was no longer to remain a sacred tongue but become a language of everyday life, of the street as much as of the house of study. What was needed, so the argument went, was a Jewish national home which would be a country like any other country. It would be a modern State in which the best of Western culture and Western democracy would be expressed in the language and terminology of the Jews. The Zionist idea set out to present Western thought in a Jewish context. The State of Israel was to epitomize it.

In terms of our paradigm – the encounter between Jacob and the guardian angel of Esau – the attempted fusion, as reflected in Reform Judaism, seems to be the most consistent, and the most authentic expression of the thrust of Jewish history. But in the light of events of the twentieth century, it is the Zionist formula – Jewish particularism based on universalist Western ideas – that has been vindicated. For with the emergence of Hitler, the Messianic vision of the Reformers turned out to be a dangerous delusion; the beautiful dream became a horrible nightmare. Not only did nation – and, in Jewish eyes, the most 'cultured' of nations, Germany – lift up sword against nation in a terrible blood bath, but six million Jews were mercilessly exterminated only because they were Jews. The openness and universalism of Reform Jews seemed now misguided. Had they been working for and settling in the Jewish national home as it was emerging in Palestine, instead of holding on to their roots in the Diaspora, not only would they have survived the Holocaust in greater numbers, but their presence and influence would have saved many others who then turned their backs on Judaism in despair.

In 1948 the State of Israel was established and many of the concentration camp survivors found a new home and a new future there. Those who put their faith in the fusion of brotherly love between Jacob and Esau saw their ideal shattered. Those who believed in peaceful co-existence in the Diaspora between Jew and Gentile were also bitterly disillusioned. But those who worked for the establishment of the Jewish State brought dignity and hope to the Jewish people.

The memory of the Holocaust and the experience of the State of Israel have both had a profound influence on all manifestations of contemporary Judaism. The majority of the ultra-Orthodox have come to reckon not only with the tragedy of the Holocaust – often avoiding glib fundamentalist 'explanations' – but also with the triumph of Israel – setting aside enough of their reservations to wish to be represented in the Israeli Cabinet. Many assimilated Jews, hitherto far removed from most things Jewish, rediscovered their true identity, both as Hitler's victims and as the builders of the new Jerusalem. Neo-Orthodoxy, with its reservations about the non-Jewish world and its strong particularist trend, has, not unexpectedly, become more articulate and determined in the light of these events and has had something of a revival in post-war America, Europe and Israel. But the most radical changes are taking place in the Reform camp. To a much greater extent than Conservative Judaism, Reform has had to reconsider its trusting universalism and has, as a result, become more particularist, both in its attitude to observance and in its affirmation of Jewish national aspirations. In this way it has come closer to the other modernist movements in Judaism.

These changes confirm us in the conviction that the encounter between Jacob and the guardian angel of Esau is a continuous process; the blessing to become Israel has to be reclaimed again and again. What follows is an attempt to indicate how this is to be done in the future. The concern of this inquiry is not any particular movement but the Jewish world as a whole. It has grown out of the conviction that for the image of Jacob – the wrestler who strives with beings divine and human in order to survive – to have meaning, more than mere survival is needed. For Judaism to survive and to have a future, it has to have a purpose. But before we can embark upon an attempt to articulate that purpose, something has to be said about the forces that currently bind and imprison Judaism.

2

The Insecurity of the Fatherless

The Biblical Jacob had to wrestle with a mysterious being in order to go forward. Prior to the momentous encounter he was immobilized. All he could do was to send emissaries to Esau and take evasive action in an effort to enable at least some of what he had achieved to survive. It is only after facing the guardian angel of Esau that he knew who he really was and was able to face the future. The discovery of his identity was linked to the realization of his purpose. The outcome was a happy one: 'Esau ran to greet him and, falling on his neck, he kissed him and they wept.'

Jacob's progress has remained the ideal model and the paradigm of Jewish history. Reality, however, has forced Jews to be suspicious of that path. For frequently the outcome was not the one envisaged by Scripture: Esau did not embrace and kiss Israel. Perhaps with this in mind, the Masoretic text has put a seemingly inexplicable dot over each of the letters of the word *vayishakehu*, 'he kissed him'. Commentators tried to explain these signs as an indication that we should not read what it says but *vayishachechu*, not 'he kissed him' but 'he bit him'. Esau is not really capable of kissing Jacob, it is implied, even when he appears to do so; what seems to be a kiss is, in fact, a bite.

The experience of the Holocaust has given new credence to this interpretation. Despite the varied efforts of the modernist movements in Judaism to meet Esau in brotherly embrace, the Holocaust provided incontrovertible evidence that the Gentile will bite even when he appears to kiss. The shock of the emancipated Jew in Europe came about not so much because he understood the political situation that made Fascism and Nazism possible, but through his discovery that seemingly liberal and fair-minded Gentiles were prepared to

lend their support, sometimes actively and sometimes pas-
sively, to the many anti-Semitic manifestations that gradually
turned the Jews into pariahs. The Holocaust seemed to have
finally buried all the ideals and aspirations that Emancipation
stood for.

One of the many effects of this shock has been a retreat
into the past. The experience of the Holocaust has made the
Jew weary of wrestling with the guardian angel of Esau.
Instead, he is anxious to consolidate his position by sitting
and waiting. Survival, not the encounter with the future,
seems to be the order of the day. Preservation of what has
been, rather than a struggle for a new identity as Israel is the
pre-occupation of the Jewish world today. Its motto is something like: 'What has been good enough for my father is good
enough for me.' To honour the memory of parents – not only
those who perished in the gas chambers but also the ancestors
from 'back home' whom we imagine to have possessed the
virtues of piety and authenticity – has become almost a religious category. When Tevye, the central character in 'Fiddler
on the Roof', explains the many facets of the life of his native
village with the single word, 'Tradition!', he is not only reflecting conditions in Czarist Russia of long ago, but expressing much of the mood among Jews living in the Western
democracies of today. Much of Jewish life today systematically
confuses religion with tradition and nostalgia with faith. The
fact that the anti-rationalist tendency in religion is currently
in fashion has, of course, provided the conducive general
climate for the specifically Jewish confusion.

The past is the fascination of every fatherless generation,
and no people has been more orphaned than we Jews. The
Holocaust has not only exterminated millions of Jewish fathers
but also rendered Jewry fatherless through the disappearance
of the many institutions that exercised authority over the
various branches of Jewish life. Having been deprived of
fatherly guidance we have been frightened into a veneration
of the past in the vain hope of finding there the direction and
the authenticity we lack. As a result, we have tended to shun
the encounter with Esau's guardian angel.

For very obvious reasons, ultra-Orthodoxy has come to
capitalize on this retreat into the past since, by its very nature,
it is dedicated to the preservation of what has been and a

rejection of what there is. It takes it for granted that the past is better than the present, because those who have lived before us were closer to the Revelation on Sinai on which Orthodoxy rests. In its scheme of things, we today are at best only dwarfs standing on the shoulders of giants of long ago who alone can carry us to the Promised Land. The retreat into the past which characterizes the post-Holocaust generation thus finds a very willing ally in the Orthodoxy that rejected Emancipation in the first place. The fact that the former is often motivated by secularist considerations in no way seems to weaken the alliance. The growth of extreme Orthodoxy is symptomatic of the insecurity in Jewish life today. The fact that Orthodoxy is also strong in the State of Israel suggests that even the Israelis are not as self-assured as it may seem.

Neo-Orthodoxy has always had to look over its 'right' shoulder to validate its claim for authenticity. In the present religious climate, therefore, it has naturally been forced into a strong anti-modernist stance as a way of claiming acceptance among the extremists. In Britain, the change of climate in the United Synagogue, the bastion of neo-Orthodoxy, has been very much in evidence in the post-war period. In Israel the difference between the tolerance of a Rav Kook, Chief Rabbi in the early days of the *Yishuv* in Palestine, and the obscurantism of Rav Goren, Israel's Chief Rabbi today, is equally marked. Neo-Orthodoxy is, therefore, in increasing measure losing its claim to be a modernist movement. At the same time, in the general swing to the 'right', Conservative Judaism in America, Reform Judaism in Britain and what is left of Liberal Judaism on the Continent of Europe prepare to take its place. The 'left' wing is moving into the 'centre' to fill the vacuum created by the swing to the 'right'.

Individuals who feel particularly abandoned and fatherless, i.e. without proper direction provided by their home, their school and their synagogue, are attracted to the regimentation and ostensible certainty of Orthodoxy. Its noisy piety and aggressive religiosity is attractive to those who wish to tell the whole world that they have at last found a spiritual haven.

The fact that Orthodoxy's veneration of the past makes it retain practices, even ways of dressing, which are different and look ancient, is an added attraction to the extrovert escapists from the here and now in their search for outward manifestations of their stance. The sight of a Jew walking to synagogue anywhere in Israel in his long black coat and fur hat on a hot summer's day offers a visual illustration of what Orthodoxy seeks to achieve. The dress was normal for East Europeans; it suited both the fashion and the climate and a couple of centuries ago was common; there is nothing especially Jewish about it. Time has given it religious status; 'because my father wore it, I must wear it too', irrespective of the fact that the climate in which I live makes fur hats unsuitable at any time of the year and wearing them has the effect of making me look hot and different. Nevertheless, young men who, by virtue of their American or European or Israeli university education could be described as modern, are drawn not only to the theology but also to the garb probably for no other reason than that it is – Tradition. Whatever their explanations may be when forced into apologetics, the real attraction seems to be precisely that it offers a paternal authenticity and so brings comfort to a fatherless generation in whom Western education has only increased the sense of insecurity and alienation. They escape into *Yeshivot*, Rabbinic academies, where the programme of study is deliberately as far removed as possible from current concerns.

Those who are tempted to embrace extreme Orthodoxy – described often as *ba'aley teshuvah*, repentants (the Jewish equivalent to 'born again'), in the special institutions in Israel and elsewhere that cater for them – constitute a small but growing minority. Combined with the fact that Orthodox families, which disapprove of birth-control, tend to be large, contemporary extreme Orthodoxy has become a formidable force, often at the expense of the 'middle of the road' alternatives. But the majority who support Orthodox institutions, extremist as well as moderate, could not themselves be described as Orthodox Jews. Frequently they do not keep the commandments that the Torah, as understood by Orthodoxy, bids them to keep, but only remember when they transgress them. Especially those who would describe themselves as atheists or agnostics have often a great need to believe in those who have faith and to support those agencies that profess it. The complaint of many rabbis serving Orthodox 'establishment' congregations is that they are hired to be pious on behalf of their non-observant congregants.

The *malaise* of vicarious piety, like the tendency in modern society to keep one's parents in comfort and isolation in purpose-built institutions, is now spreading to Conservative and Reform communities which, by and large, tend to be more successful the more 'right-wing' they appear to be – always on the understanding, of course, that nothing beyond a subscription is actually demanded from the members themselves. The spiritual leader who finds it uncomfortable to collude in this manner, by either refusing to be more pious or 'traditional' than his congregants or by seeking to impose his standards on them, runs the risk of not having his contract renewed. Much of the religious physiognomy of contemporary Jewry in the Diaspora is decided by professional Jews who need secure and well-paid jobs and get them by offering what the 'customers' want. If that state of affairs continues, there is a great danger that the whole of Diaspora Jewry will be sapped of its vitality and reduced to a quaint museum piece by those who practise Judaism, and a depository of religious memories by those who support the system.

3

Israeli Necrophilia

It is obvious why this should be the case in the Diaspora. There the Jew cannot avoid being confronted with the insecurities of assimilation and anti-Semitism, which are peculiarly his and have remained so to this day, and the trauma of alienation, which he shares with his non-Jewish neighbour in America, Europe and elsewhere where modernity has taken hold. In that confusion the distant past, and those who reflect it today, seem to offer certainties. But that it should be so in Israel, too, where – so it seems, at least – the Jew can remain Jewish without the accompanying neuroses (even if he cannot be shielded from the alienation caused by modern technological society), is remarkable. The escape into tradition in search of a father-substitute on the part of the Diaspora Jew can be explained by the fact that he was orphaned at Auschwitz, but why does the Israeli Jew follow the same escape route? The question is not only of theoretical interest, but has immediate practical, political consequences. For if the belief that only the past contains the truth continues to permeate Israeli life, the Jewish State is in danger of being reduced to an Ayatolla-style theocracy in which the religious fanatics will have the real power and the non-observant majority will be fed on the mixture of mythology and nostalgia that it so greatly craves. That the tendency towards this kind of collusion between the fanatically committed fringe and the frantically searching centre is real in Israel is attested to by the fact that every government since the inception of the Jewish State has been dependent on the Orthodox political parties to a far greater extent than their support in the polling booths would indicate.

To begin with, the pioneers who shaped the Jewish State could combine their avowed opposition to religious Judaism with a marked tolerance of Jewish Orthodoxy because the latter, by being so different and so quaint, provided a suitable illustration of why modern man, the modern Jew, should have nothing to do with religion. By appearing unreasonable, vulgar and politicized, Orthodoxy provided a much needed caricature of religion that could persuade the majority of the Jewish population of what was then Palestine that religion was not for them; that it was an outmoded relic of the Diaspora they had abandoned.

By now, that which may have started as a ploy has become something more. Whereas in its early stages Zionism was presented as the modern revolutionary nationalist movement it undoubtedly is, in our days it is described more and more as the adaptation of the age-old yearning for Zion, the application of tradition and not a break with it. The shift from the revolutionary image to the traditionalist one cannot be understood merely as the realization that Judaism in the last resort cannot be secularized, because it knows of no distinction between 'religious' and 'secular'. It is not only the result of the recognition that Judaism is a civilization comprising the totality of man's experience and that Zionism, therefore, must be seen from that perspective. For had the quest been merely to rediscover the 'religious' dimension in the 'secular' Zionist enterprise, surely non-Orthodox Judaism would have been the more suitable vehicle. In fact, however, both Conservative and Reform Judaism have been virtually ignored in the Jewish State, although their exponents, for all their American accents, are no more alien in Israel than the Orthodox fanatics in Jerusalem's Orthodox quarter, *Mea Shearim*. The fascination with Orthodoxy on the part of those Israelis who describe themselves as secularists cannot be understood properly unless we see it as an escape route into the past.

Even more significant than the Israelis' rejection of Reform and Conservative Judaism is their rejection of one of the great thinkers of our generation who lived the last three decades of his life in their midst: Martin Buber. He affirmed Zionist aspirations almost from the outset and viewed them in the context of his understanding of Judaism. But his emphasis on the here and now as the stuff out of which reality is shaped, his radical critique of the past and his disdain for Orthodoxy made him unacceptable. Buber seriously challenged the escape mechanisms and, therefore, was ignored. His reluctance to find his Judaism in the past may have also had something to do with the fact that he was a witness to the disastrous effect that the glorification of the past had on the German people, generating a reactionary mood which could, in the end, adapt even to National Socialism.

Had Martin Buber lived today he would have been horrified at the turn to right-wing politics both by Jews in the Diaspora and now by a growing proportion of Israel's population. In Israel those on the political right-wing, be they Orthodox or not, very often use the past – the Bible, archaeology, historical precedent – to legitimize their extremist actions as yet another manifestation of the escape into the past, with disastrous effects for the present and the future.

Even the interest in archaeology, so prevalent in the Jewish State, must be viewed in this context. It is an attempt to bring material proof as scientific evidence for the incontrovertible superiority of the past and our duty to emulate it. The attraction to extreme Orthodoxy and the fascination with digging up the past stem from the same wish to avoid the present and indulge in culturally, not clinically, what Erich Fromm has described as necrophilia, which he sees as 'malignant aggression' and identifies with the love of the past:

> For the necrophilous character only the past is experienced as quite real, not the present or the future. What has been, i.e., what is dead, rules his life: institutions, laws, property, traditions, and possessions. Briefly, *things rule man*; *having* rules *being*; *the dead* rule *the living*. In the necrophile's thinking – personal, philosophical, and political – the past is sacred, nothing new is valuable, drastic change is a crime against the 'natural' order.[1]

For all its modernity, Messianic vision and dependence on science and technology, Israel has not yet been able to wrestle with the guardian angel of Esau. Its pre-occupation is with the past, as manifest in such seemingly different phenomena as veneration of Orthodoxy and fascination with archaeology.

---

[1] Erich Fromm, *The Anatomy of Human Destructiveness* (Penguin 1977), p. 451.

4

Neurotic Existence

In view of the domination of Israel over Jewish life and the
hankering for the past on the part of many Jews, it is understandable that non-Orthodox religious Judaism has been
caught in the same trap, despite all its protestations of liberalism and future-orientation. Both Reform and Conservative
Judaism have also tended to escape into the past. That is
obviously more easily done in the Conservative *ambiance*, with
its stress on 'historic Judaism', but spokesmen of Reform
Judaism proclaim themselves to be the heirs of both the
Prophets and the Pharisees, and see their principal aim as the
preservation of their teachings. Even these ostensibly inno-
vative movements insist, in the last resort, that they are mere
links in the chain of tradition that started with Moses. The
literature they produce frequently plays down the revolutionary dimension of their enterprise by insisting that they only
continue what the Bible and the Talmud started. Not without
good reason do they accuse Orthodoxy of the obscurantism
that has arrested Jewish development in its medieval mould
which they, the innovators, have come to liberate and restore
to its pristine glory. But they fail to see their own inability to
face the future without the protection, and imprisonment, of
the past.

Conservative and Reform Judaism go back, of course, to
the glorification of the past reflected in *Wissenschaft des Ju-
dentums*, 'the science of Judaism', which sought to legitimize
the change in the present by bringing evidence from the past.
Although, as Peter Gay has written, 'even Jewish historians
[of the nineteenth century] concentrating on the Jewish past,
extraordinarily sensitive to their surviving parochialism, did
their utmost to imitate the documentary obsession of Momm-

sen and the Olympian detachment of Ranke,' [1] it was more than mere imitation of the German academic tradition. As such it was a noble enterprise which opened the eyes of Jewish scholarship to new dimensions of our rich and varied heritage. Its exponents included men who in their own religious endeavours were revolutionaries, e.g. Abraham Geiger, the true founder of Reform Judaism, and Samuel Holdheim, one of its more radical exponents. For them the new dimension of Jewish scholarship and their new discoveries of religious life were of the same ilk, but their successors have often reduced scholarship (in)to antiquarianism. Following Buber's paradigm, that which started as an *I–thou* experience of authentic learning has become an *I–it* chore of derivative scholarship. The vitality that the original impetus of *Wissenschaft* brought to non-Orthodox Judaism has gone. Those who now cling to it do so for the same reasons that others dig for archaeological finds and others again lose themselves in Talmudic casuistry, to evade the present and the future through pre-occupation with the past.

The pursuit of Jewish scholarship as an escape mechanism is nowadays by no means the prerogative of Reform and Conservative Judaism, although the Rabbinic seminaries that both have created tend to regard themselves as the natural and legitimate heirs of the science of Judaism. Today, both Orthodox Jews and Jewish secularists are equal partners in that enterprise, and the non-Jewish world has joined in. Although, no doubt, it is Jewish influence and Jewish money that has prompted many American universities to establish Judaica departments, their phenomenal growth cannot be solely attributed to these. There seems to be a widespread interest in promoting Jewish scholarship. On the face of it, there is every reason to welcome this development, but that does not mean that we should ignore the wider implications: another manifestation of the flight into the past, this time in the very respectable guise of academia.

The non-Jewish world supports the flight for its own reasons. Christians have, of course, always been able to tolerate Judaism only as a relic from the past, an earlier stage of

[1] Peter Gay, *Freud, Jews and Other Germans* (Oxford University Press 1979), p. 99.

religious development now rendered obsolete by Christianity. To this very day there is a great demand on Jewish speakers to address Christian audiences on the symbols and rituals of Judaism. These audiences are fascinated by all quaint expressions of Jewish religiosity because, as their spokesmen so frequently testify in their profuse votes of thanks, 'it helps us to understand how our Lord lived and why he had to do what he did'. Christians thus encourage Jews to escape into the past out of their own Christological needs. When Jews are not available, Christians themselves sometimes present Judaism in this way. In Germany, for example, where it is difficult to find Jewish speakers, baptized Jews and Christian missionaries have often been deployed in this task. Much of the work of the Council of Christians and Jews there, as well as in Britain and other countries, is devoted to providing this kind of picture of Judaism. Audiences appear to be less interested in genuine Jewish–Christian dialogue and seem to be irritated by every presentation of Judaism as a living faith, concerned with the here and now, in the language of the here and now. Similarly, the secular society in which Jews live, and which so often has its thinly disguised residue of Christian prejudices, finds it easier to tolerate historic scholarship about Jews and Judaism, confined to obscure university departments, than to respond to living and thriving Jewish religious communities.

Escape into the past, fostered by internal Jewish neuroses, is being reinforced by non-Jewish prejudices. The Jewish world thus deludes itself into a belief that it helps to protect and preserve Judaism – it sees the stress on the past as the most important tool in the struggle for Jewish survival – and the Gentile world is being duped to regard its support of this endeavour as a sign of its tolerance and broadmindedness. Although it may appear ungracious to express criticism of both, it has to be done if the future of Judaism is to be safeguarded. For ultimately Judaism cannot exist, let alone survive, under the motto, 'What was good enough for my father is good enough for me.' Instead it must evolve towards a formula that says, 'What is good enough for my children is good enough for me.' To seek to transmit Judaism by escaping into the past is not only neurotic but, in the long term, totally ineffective. If it works at all, it only does so to a generation still traumatized by the Holocaust and not yet at home – partly because of the Holocaust – in the world at large. The flight into the past is only a transitory stage, both in Israel and in the Diaspora; if we are to take Judaism seriously we must change its emphasis into an exploration of its future.

This must never mean, of course, that we ignore the past. On the contrary, the first argument in favour of staying Jewish, as I have stated it in the Preface, is that we are a link in the chain of a remarkable history. We must learn from that history and interpret it as a prerequisite to our own self-understanding. History is not something to escape into but to develop from. Thus understood it ceases to be a mere description of the past, and becomes the frame of reference by which the present and the future are to make sense. It ceases to be mere archivism and becomes theology. A perception of Jewish history which recognizes the value of the past and the importance to study it, and yet refuses to be imprisoned by it, forms the basis of a theological understanding of Judaism.

II

THE SURVIVAL SYNDROME
Suffering without Despair

> To survive, one had to want to survive for a purpose.
>
> Bruno Bettelheim[1]

> Survivors should have the decency to refrain from supplying the easy answers with which they so often assuage their guilt for surviving.
>
> Peter Gay[2]

---

[1] Bruno Bettelheim, *Surviving and Other Essays* (Thames and Hudson 1979), p. 293.
[2] Peter Gay, *Freud, Jews and Other Germans* (Oxford University Press 1979), p. 163.

5

A Faith Forged by Foes

Escaping into the past prevents the contemporary Jew from responding adequately to the needs of the present. This is reflected in all movements in Judaism today and especially manifest in our educational institutions and policies. We begin, therefore, this chapter with some reflections on Jewish education today.

In Orthodoxy, be it 'extreme' or 'moderate', the escapism is reflected in its preoccupation with the minutiae of the Law, through which the past allegedly speaks with unquestionable authority to each Jew, young and old. Orthodoxy's educational framework, therefore, functions with relatively little regard for the actual religious needs of those who are sent to its institutions of learning, for only a small number are *ba'aley teshuvah*, converts to Orthodoxy, who have found their own way to it; the majority are conditioned from birth.

In Israel it is not Zionism, the modernist movement which brought about the Jewish State, that fires the imagination of many of her citizens, but archaeology. Once again it is interest in the past, not the present, that dominates. In his quest for 'hard' evidence of Israelite possession of the Land, the Israeli pupil is moved by the tangible exhibits, but bored with the message contained in Jewish studies.

The non-Orthodox framework of Jewish education in the Diaspora, although in theory not imprisoned by the past, but open to the present and the future, in practice is only effective when it plays on the glorification of the past, notably through the ceremony of *Barmitsvah*. It is on the relatively low demands in terms of actual knowledge and on the panache for decorum and 'production' that Reform and Conservative synagogues thrive in the Diaspora. *Barmitsvah* reflects both. Without a *Barmitsvah*, most synagogues are empty, many do not even hold Shabbat morning services. The stress on this relatively unimportant, but sociologically significant, relic of earlier times has made many Jews, who want the past without really practising Judaism, flock into non-Orthodox synagogues, and out of fear of competition, many neo-Orthodox congregations have come to imitate their less than kosher rivals.

The almost universal interest in *Barmitsvah* among Jews, expressed by Diaspora assimilationists as much as by Israeli secularists, offers an apt illustration of this nostalgia for the past, without much concern for either the present or the future. Despite the fact that the ceremony is relatively recent in Jewish history, and in its present form quite insignificant, contemporary Jews have vested it with tremendous importance. Many explanations are offered for this, but most of them amount to a recognition of the desire to link the child to that which has been without necessarily committing him to what ought to be. Surely, other factors are also at play – e.g. its similarity to a puberty rite for boys; the socio-economic factors that make middle class parents look for an occasion to give a party for the son in compensation for the fact that one day they will have to pay for his sister's wedding; the last opportunity that parents have to impose their will on a child – but these seem to be less important than the general desire to conform to 'tradition'. Thus in most cases the boys stop their religious education immediately after *Barmitsvah* and are frequently only trained for that ceremony, with neither intention nor opportunity to learn much else. And the girls receive even less Jewish education, since 'tradition' does not require them to have a corresponding ceremony.

Jewish parents foolishly believe that, once they have linked their son to the chain of 'tradition', his and their survival as Jews is guaranteed. They see no reason to foster the Jewish commitment of their children, especially if it in any way interferes with their secular activities. At the same time they will willingly support institutions, notably those aiding Israel, which appear to safeguard survival, and maintain tradition. Even when parents act in a manner calculated to expose their children to anti-Semitism and assimilation, e.g. by sending them to 'establishment' boarding schools in England, they will insist that they are committed to remaining Jewish. Often the very act of anti-Semitism evokes in them the desire to survive as Jews, but without any attempt to secure Jewish continuity through meaningful Jewish education and a Jewish life-style.

When I expressed disapproval to a member of the congregation I serve of his sending his son to a boarding school he 'reassured' me that I had nothing to worry about for 'he knows that he is Jewish'. I probed: 'Does he do any studying of Jewish sources?' – 'No, he is too busy with school work, sport and the other activities that reflect successful integration into school life.' I asked again: 'Is he able to observe anything of Jewish life?' The answer was not unexpected: 'Of course not. How would that be possible in a Christian foundation? In fact he has to go to chapel daily.' I persevered: 'In what way, then, does your son know that he is Jewish beyond the obvious fact that he was born a Jew?' Answer: 'He encounters anti-Semitism almost daily and has to fight the boys who tease him because he is a Jew.' It is to this that Jewish identity has been reduced in the eyes of many, not a manifestation of a positive commitment but a defence mechanism.

Even the very welcome growth of Jewish Day Schools does not seem to have altered the situation radically. That the children of very Orthodox families – who are most likely to go to Jewish Day Schools – stay in the fold is not surprising; that some other ex-pupils of Jewish schools are more motivated to emigrate to Israel and thus, almost by definition, remain Jewish, should also be conceded. But it is a sad fact that a large proportion of those who have had a full-time Jewish education nevertheless do not regard Judaism as central to their lives. Only when attacked by anti-Semites does their will to survive reassert itself, and that does not appear in any way to be the result of their schooling but the outcome of other causes. Very often children of non-Orthodox parents are being sent to Jewish schools for negative reasons: because the neighbourhood is too 'run down' and thus the local school unsuitable; or because the Jewish Day School is cheaper than the local Church school; or because no other school would have the child.

Judaism as a negative reaction, rather than a positive programme, is being instilled in the children from a very early age. It is this that militates against their Jewish commitment in adult life. Whereas the escape into the past may offer some comfort to the middle-aged, it is less certain that it will be sufficiently attractive to the young. It is not at all sure that even survival will be that important to them. When confronted with anti-Jewish prejudices, they may either explain them away – the ploy of liberals – or accept them – the psychopathology of all self-hating Jews. Stress on survival as a response to persecution may very well breed assimilation in the next generation.

The fact that religious education has ceased to matter in our state educational system, and that the gap between public morality and private conduct in our society is very wide, further legitimize the double standard reflected in the Jewish paradox. However, in order to understand what is happening in the Jewish world, we must recognize the Jewish propensity to escape into the past – which absolves us from offering our children guidance for the present – and, secondly, take into account the fact that most Jews today regard themselves as survivors. Survival, therefore, has become a precious Jewish heritage, something of a sacred cow. It works for those who are now adults; it is less likely to work for their children and grandchildren.

Because it was not for the victims in the camps and the crematoria to decide whether they would survive or not, those who remained after the end of the Hitler era, and their children, felt a special obligation to carry on. But at the same time the endeavour to build up their personal lives in the post-war period and to succeed financially and socially by being integrated into the general secular society, has left them with little time and even less inclination for Jewish life and Jewish studies. Psychologists might also identify an inertia caused by mixed feelings, a sense of duty to carry on Judaism and a deep resentment at having been landed with it in the first place. The 'compromise' has been to limit one's personal Judaism to a minimum, but to insist on collective survival.

By supporting Jewish institutions of all kinds, not least extremist Orthodox establishments, the survivors and their children believed that continuity would be guaranteed. These institutions, in turn, by providing ways of escaping into an almost mythical past, found ways of colluding with their benefactors without demanding much of them. Such collusion has

been particularly in evidence among camp survivors whose
assimilation has often proceeded at an incredible pace, and
whose children have even less real Jewish commitment than
other Jews of similar age. To understand this fully we must
await further analysis of the so-called survivor syndrome with
its 'consequent sense of alienation, isolation and inability to
trust or form relationships' [1] and the effect all this has had on
the victims' self-understanding as Jews. But what can be
stated already now – and this is one of the contentions of this
book – is that contemporary Judaism is the victim of a *survival*
syndrome, i.e. that it seems unable to offer a positive reason
for staying Jewish but at the same time is neurotically pre-
occupied with the danger of ceasing to be Jewish. The relative
failure of Jewish education is a manifestation of this syndrome. It seeks to offer easy answers to assuage the guilt of
survivors, but fails, for such guilt is rarely inherited by their
children and grandchildren.

It is as if we Jews could not cope with the success of our
endeavours to assimilate. In the same way as persecution
destroys us physically, tolerance tends to demoralize us
psychologically. What we are looking for is a kind of compromise between the concentration camp and the public school,
and we find it often enough in the latent and overt anti-
Semitism in Western society. The only way, as it were, by
which we can seek assimilation and survival at the same time
is if the Western world sets limits on our integration and
penalizes us for our Jewish origins. And as long as this is also
felt by our children, their allegiance to ˙Judaism can be
counted upon. The anti-Semitism that exists in the countries
where Jews live as equal citizens is, ironically, a kind of
safeguard for Jewish continuity. However neurotic and self-
destructive we Jews may be about our Judaism, our foes make
sure that we remain Jewish.

In the classical epoch of assimilation, in nineteenth century
Germany, 'waves of anti-Semitism made wavelets of conversion; times of calm reduced the urge to join the safety of the
dominant denominations'.[2] But that was at a time when

---

[1] Gill Pyrah, 'The Survivor Syndrome', *The Listener* 16 August 1979,
p. 200.
[2] Peter Gay, *op. cit.*, p. 97.

religion still mattered and before Hitler's racialism had demonstrated the futility of the effort. In our age wavelets of anti-Semitism appear to produce waves of collective Jewish allegiance, albeit of a neurotic variety. That is an irony of contemporary history and suggests that, perhaps, even anti-Semites have a vested interest in continued Jewish existence. Whom would they scapegoat otherwise? Even Hitler, it can be argued, only decided to exterminate the Jews when he had nowhere to expel them.

Whether there is an unconscious bond between persecutor and persecuted or not, there is little doubt that the presence of anti-Semitism in the world furthers the cause of Jewish group survival and is a force for unity and solidarity. This is evident each time neo-Nazi parties emerge on the political arena; it is also evident in relation to the persecution of Jews in the Soviet Union, in Muslim countries and, indeed, anywhere in the world. The attacks on synagogues in Paris and Vienna in 1980 and 1981 had a revivifying effect on many Jewish communities throughout the world, despite the resources they had to deploy to tighten security arrangements. Because the experience of Germany is fresh in our minds, we Jews are, of course, especially sensitive to any resurgence of those forces that destroyed a third of our people. But, if we delve a little deeper into our motives, we find that by identifying anti-Semitism we are, somehow, let off the hook. We no longer have to worry that much about Jewish education, about whether we sentimentalize our Judaism and escape into a mythical past, whether we are neurotic about survival – all that matters now is that we defend ourselves. It is, therefore, not surprising that emigration and even tourism to Israel, as well as financial support of the Jewish State, increase in proportion to the danger felt. By functioning under – real or imaginary – emergency conditions, we need not concern ourselves too much about the theological basis of our Judaism.

The most telling illustration of this is perhaps the emergence of vigilante groups in the suburbs of all cities with a sizeable Jewish population to defend the synagogues and to protect institutions. Men who would not enter a synagogue even on the Day of Atonement, the holiest day in the Jewish calendar, will gallantly stand *outside* it by day or by night to protect it from possible intruders and arsonists. Jews who have no particular regard for what the Scrolls of the Law contain will give up time and energy to make sure that they are secure. True, the image of Nazis desecrating sacred Scrolls haunts many Jews, but perhaps other reasons are behind their solicitude, too: it is easier to stand outside a synagogue than to pray within it; it is easier to fight for survival in the sight of enemies than to pray for it in the presence of God. Even in Israel where Jews so heroically sacrifice their lives for the Jewish people, a lasting peace may uncover a spiritual *malaise* that is too frightening even to contemplate. Sadat was wrong when he thought that by attacking Israel on the Day of Atonement in 1973 her Jews would be in synagogue; in fact, most of them were asleep.

A faith that is only expressed when the enemy attacks, and not when God calls man to prayer and atonement, is a faith forged by foes. There is much to suggest that the survival syndrome, which so strongly dominates contemporary Jewish life, is based on such faith. It is this that makes Jewish existence and Jewish thought so precarious in our time. A vision of the future must, therefore, begin with a radical understanding of the present condition and an almost ruthless determination to change it. If survival is not to be at the mercy of our adversaries, it must be based on a sense of Jewish purpose. Even in the concentration camps, where life and death were totally dependent on the camp commanders, to know that one's existence had meaning helped many an inmate to endure and to survive. How much more is this true in our generation!

6

Hitler's Posthumous Victory

And yet, despite our impatience with the stress on survival as an escape from responsibility for authentic Jewish education, and notwithstanding our despondency with the grotesque manifestations of it in the community, we must beware of too strict a castigation of the agnostic and atheist parents of bewildered children, who seek to cover up their inadequacies by fighting real or imaginary anti-Semitism. They, we all, live in the shadow of the Holocaust. We are perplexed by it; our lack of faith stems from it – as does our determination to survive and to prevent another Auschwitz. In this we must seek the clue to our reaction, to our over-reaction.

Remembering how the world refused to see the danger of German Nazism in the 1920s and 1930s, we have become over-sensitive to signs and portents. Perhaps we find it even futile to teach our children Jewish values when a pogrom can destroy them; the Jewish communities in Eastern Europe before the Holocaust had the right educational policy – and look what happened to their children within a few years! That is why not only the boy in his school but also the father in his office find their Judaism in self-defence. It is their way of expiating the sin of inactivity of earlier generations and a protest against 'proper' upbringing in a less than proper world. That is why even those who doubt the intrinsic merits of the ancient teachings are driven to defend them; that is why even if they do not believe in what Judaism stands for, their sense of outrage at what the Nazis did to us demands that Judaism survive. It is a neurotic reaction, but nevertheless a response that we have to acknowledge and take seriously, even if ultimately we must reject it. For much of Jewish life can only be understood from the vantage point of this neurosis and, if we wish to cure it, we must, in the first instance, try to comprehend it.

The survival syndrome has found its theological underpinning in the writings of Emil Fackenheim. This is how he describes his 'conversion':

> I confess I used to be highly critical of Jewish philosophies which seemed to advocate no more than survival for survival's sake. I have changed my mind. I now believe that, in this present, unbelievable age, even a mere collective commitment to Jewish group survival for its own sake is a momentous response, with the greatest implications. I am convinced that future historians will understand it, not, as our present detractors would have it, as the tribal response-mechanism of a fossil, but rather as a profound, albeit as yet fragmentary, act of faith, in an age of crisis to which the response might well have been either flight in total disarray or complete despair.[1]

The change of heart induced Fackenheim to suggest that an additional commandment should be added to the traditional system of Jewish observance: 'The authentic Jew of today is forbidden to hand Hitler yet another, posthumous victory.' [2] Much of his thinking, including his affirmation of Zionism and the State of Israel, has been an application of that principle, an expression of what he regards as the 614th Commandment (in addition to the 613 identified by *Halacha*). The question is, of course, whether it is an authentic reflection of Jewish theology or a mere attempt to elevate the neurotic clamour for survival to a respectable doctrine. It is a haunting question. Whatever we do in the future as a people and as a community of faith will depend on the answer.

It has already been stated that Jewish existence is constantly threatened both by anti-Semitism and by assimilation. Therefore, the question of Jewish survival is important, for there can be no Judaism without Jews and the self-exclusion of assimilated Jews from the Jewish community may turn out to be as damaging to God's purpose as their extermination at the

---

[1] Emil L. Fackenheim, 'Jewish Values in the Post-Holocaust Future' a symposium in *Judaism*, xvi, 3 (Summer 1967), p. 271.
[2] ibid., p. 272.

hands of their enemies. We have already considered the gruesome prospect of anti-Semitism aiding in some way the struggle for Jewish survival. Let us now look at the effect of
assimilation on the prospects for contemporary Jewry. For as
much as anti-Semitism continues to be a threat to Judaism,
it is also a force which in some absurd way helps many
marginal Jews to retain their Jewish identity. Assimilation,
on the other hand, does not possess the same 'fail safe' mechanism, and since it has been easier for individuals and for
groups to merge into the general secular community, the
danger to Jewish survival posed by friends may be greater
than that inherent in the machinations of foes.

The irony of this state of affairs should not escape us. Since
the Emancipation, the greatest hope of individual Jews as well
as of many movements in Judaism has been successful integration into the surrounding society. As this objective is being
achieved, so we are becoming alarmed, because the price of
the achievement is the weakening of the 'guardian angel of
Esau', as described in the previous chapter, and not the increased tenacity and resourcefulness of Jacob. Because the
spiritual component of Western civilization has become so
very much weaker in recent decades and reduced itself to a
vague secular mass culture, it has become very much easier
for the Jew to become part of it. But, at the same time, the
Jew is entering that society stripped of his identity, because
he did not have to wrestle for it. The elimination of the
struggle has deprived him of the blessing.

The modern Jew finds himself, therefore, in a seemingly
self-contradictory situation. On the one hand, he is always at
risk as a target for anti-Semitism and as such subject to a kind
of neurosis, but, on the other, he finds it relatively easy to
merge with the society in which he lives and remain 'unde-
tected' as a Jew, simply because fewer people care for religion
or 'ethnicity'. However, he never quite knows how it is going
to work out, and that only further increases both his insecurity
and his neurosis.

If the attitude to *Barmitsvah* is indicative of the Jewish
notion of survival, the attitude to intermarriage reflects the
insecurity and the neurosis. It may be useful to discuss it in
this context as an illustration of the dilemma. Intermarriage
is today a universal phenomenon in the Jewish world; even

Israeli kibbutzim which receive non-Jewish volunteer workers
have been affected by it. Only the ultra-Orthodox groupings,
because of their fundamentalist outlook and inner cohesive-
ness are free from it.

One of the many benefits of Emancipation is access to
universities in the countries where Jews live, as well as to
places of work and leisure. It is, therefore, inevitable that
when Jews and non-Jews mix freely, some of them will wish
to marry each other. One of the ironies of human existence
is that we tend to be attracted to people who are different
from us, although our chances of forming stable and lasting
relationships are greatest with people of similar outlook and
background. The result is that many young Jews and Jewesses
find non-Jewish marriage partners. The fact that your partner
belongs to the group of your former, present or potential,
persecutors only increases the attraction. It is remarkable, for
example, how many concentration camp survivors married
'Aryan' Germans and had not marriage laws in Israel been
what they are today, marriages between Jew and Arab would
have been not uncommon.

To this yet another factor has to be added: marrying 'out'
is a Jew's conscious, or unconscious, way of opting out of
Judaism. Even if he, or she, cannot entirely cease to be Jewish, because the outside world will not let them, the children
of mixed marriages are more likely to have that opportunity.
True, Hitler applied racialist criteria which made even that
impossible, but few believe that the pseudo-scientific theories
on which he based his programme will be resurrected in the
future. Therefore, intermarriage becomes a realistic way of
leaving the fold and joining the majority group, which (often
only by implication but sometimes deliberately) has been the
cause of the Jew's miserable minority status.

In practice, of course, it is not as simple as that. For
although parents in mixed marriages may dream of an anti-
septic secular upbringing for their children, sometimes even
deluding themselves that the young will be able to choose
freely, in real life the children are either brought up as Christians – to the chagrin of the Jewish parent, who may have
wished that his child escape Judaism, but not that he embrace
Christianity – or burdened with all the unresolved problems
of father and mother. If there is such a thing as a survivor

syndrome, there may also be a mixed marriage syndrome, and innocent children are its real victims.

In theory, at least, this latter syndrome would not exist for those families who live in Israel. In practice, it is the other way around. Although the absence of the institution of civil marriage makes mixed marriages impossible in the country itself, when mixed marriage families wish to settle in the Jewish State – as for example, refugees from the Soviet Union – they encounter numerous difficulties caused by the domination of the Orthodox Chief Rabbinate over Israeli life. We are thus left with yet another irony: the place which should guarantee Jewish survival for all, is also the place which makes such survival impossible for those most exposed to Jewish extinction. Neither does living in Israel automatically guarantee a commitment to Jewish marriage. Reference to non-Jewish kibbutz volunteers has already been made. The presence of a large number of Israelis in Western countries, many of whom are married to non-Jews, is further evidence.

The Jewish community is, not unexpectedly, alarmed by the ever growing proportion of its children – in a decreasing birth rate – leaving the fold. The children of those who did not perish at Auschwitz, or some other camp, may now cease to be Jews as they graduate from Oxford or some other campus. It is a devastating shock to the exponents of Emancipation that both towns may have the same effect on the future of Judaism. To have to fight Emancipation the way we had to fight extermination is distasteful, but it may nevertheless be necessary, unless Hitler is to have his posthumous victory.

The fight against Emancipation has, however, already begun on the part of those who profess to care for the future of Judaism. It is manifest in the growing disdain for Western culture and in the growing attraction of extremist Orthodoxy. Both are misguided for they aim at separation in place of integration and because they evade the real challenge: the encounter between Jacob and the 'guardian angel of Esau'. Nevertheless it is an understandable phenomenon, for Western civilization, be it in its most degenerate form at Auschwitz or even in its most noble expression at Oxford, constitutes a threat to the future of Judaism and, therefore, evokes a shrill and almost hysterical, call for survival. To disapprove and to condemn is insufficient, unless we can offer a viable alternative to the very real danger that Hitler may get his posthumous victory.

7

Strategies for Survival

Before we attempt an outline of how the future of Judaism can be safeguarded without the present neurotic efforts, we must seek to describe and identify the strategies currently used. By its very nature the description will concentrate on organized Jewry rather than on the endeavours of individuals. Once again we return to the headings applied earlier in this book: Orthodoxy, Reform (incorporating Liberal and Conservative Judaism) and Zionism. The attempts at assimilation have already been alluded to, and, in any case, it cannot be described as a strategy for survival, but its opposite. It is the view that assimilation is both undesirable (a failure to struggle with 'the guardian angel of Esau'; a way of giving Hitler a posthumous victory) and ineffective (causing confusion without bringing about a solution) that has prompted the three streams of Jewish life to develop alternative approaches.[1]

The Orthodox strategy is maximum isolation from the surrounding culture. Separate schools and separate social activities for men and women of all ages is part of it. It is significant that in its current apologetic and propagandist literature it has relatively little to say about obedience to the will of God, as manifest in His word (the Torah), but much about the cohesive power of tradition and observance as reflected in the Orthodox lifestyle. It believes itself to be the most reliable

---

[1] I have chosen to ignore a fourth approach that emerged in the 19th century and was annihilated by Hitler: the approach of non-Zionist Jewish secularists, coupled with the *Bund* organization. Its history is of some interest, but its impact on contemporary Jewish life, alas, non-existent. It is one of the many casualties of the Holocaust. The fact that it disappeared so totally may have been in its very nature: a Judaism grounded on neither faith nor land but merely on 'culture' can only be a transient phenomenon.

guarantor of Jewish survival in the face of assimilation. Its opponents are consistently being branded as assimilationists, at best misguided but often malevolent fifth columnists standing on the moving staircase to Christianity or secularism.

Another device of Orthodoxy in the service of Jewish survival is the encouragement of large families. Since Jewish law, as understood by Orthodoxy, frowns upon birth control, this is natural. The ecological argument does not come into it on the basis that we Jews have a special responsibility to compensate for the six million that perished in the Holocaust. One way of not giving Hitler a posthumous victory is to make sure that many Jewish children are born.

The problem of the Jewish birth rate is a serious one. According to a recent estimate the average number of children in a Jewish family in Britain is 1.71, which is a contributory factor to the steady decline in the number of Jews affiliated to a synagogue.[2] Even the Jewish birth rate in Israel is said to be giving cause for alarm, since it is very much lower than that of the Arab population under Israeli jurisdiction. The question of birth control, therefore, assumes theological significance in the context of Jewish survival.

What a liberal theologian like Fackenheim may express as a formula (the imperative to survive), the Orthodox Jew practises in his own life through strict and separatist observance, which includes the negation of birth control. Although there are different levels of Orthodoxy and not all Jews who describe themselves as Orthodox are consistently observant, this has nevertheless remained the ideal. It has been very effective, and today the more extremist Orthodox groups grow at a greater rate than any other movement in Judaism. In fact, at a time when the Jewish population in the Diaspora is on the decline, extreme Orthodoxy is on the increase.

It is significant that the same opponents that Orthodox spokesmen describe as assimilationist and dangerous to Jewish survival – Reform and Liberal Judaism in Britain, Conservative and Reform Judaism in the United States, Liberal Judaism on the Continent of Europe – all seek to legitimize their existence with arguments similar to those of Orthodoxy. They

[2] Jane Moonman, *Anglo Jewry* (The Joint Israel Appeal, London 1980), p. 13.

often claim that they are able to reach sections of the community not accessible to other groups. Through their open and undogmatic understanding of Jewish law and their tolerance with regard to Jewish observance they claim to make Judaism accessible and easy to the Jew who wishes to live in the open society and yet, for whatever reasons, retain some links with Judaism. These modernist movements all marshal impressive evidence in support of their claim, and it is probably true that without them a substantial proportion of world Jewry would have been totally lost to Judaism.

The attitude to mixed marriages is a case in point. Whereas the exclusiveness of Orthodox society and its rigid interpretation of Jewish law tend to isolate the Jew who marries a non-Jewish spouse and alienate him, or her, from Judaism, Conservative, Reform and Liberal Judaism make it relatively easy for the non-Jewish partner to embrace Judaism. Orthodoxy tends to punish the 'sinner' who marries 'out'; the others tend to welcome his spouse by making an affirmation of Judaism possible. In some circles in Reform Judaism in the United States, making it easy includes not demanding even formal conversion; there are a number of rabbis who officiate at marriages between Jews and non-Jews in the hope that their children will remain Jewish. It is not my intention here to evaluate this approach, but only to record it as yet another strategy in the fight for Jewish survival.

Our opinion as to whether Orthodoxy or Reform is the true force that makes for Jewish survival will depend, of course, on our basic religious outlook. If we are fundamentalists, affirming that the Law of Moses is basically immutable and tradition possesses total authority, we will opt for the former. If, on the other hand, we are modernists and see the Torah as an inspired human response to God's self-disclosure to the people Israel, and tradition as having 'a vote but not a veto' we will seek to defend the Reform position. I will argue in a later chapter in favour of the modernist position, but that is not to say that I do not recognize the force of the Orthodox strategy, even though I am not able to affirm its basic assumptions. In the struggle for Jewish survival every attempt that helps the Jew to retain his Judaism should be encouraged.

Whether Orthodox or Reform, many Jews will argue that Zionism and its creation, the State of Israel, is a most potent force in the endeavour to rescue Jews from assimilation. Hitler finally vindicated Zionism. Orthodoxy before the Second World War was rich in liturgical expressions of yearning for Zion, but largely indifferent to the aspirations of political Zionism. Reform, with its belief that the brotherhood of man, epitomized by the modern Western State, would bring in the Messianic era often led to outright hostility to Zionism. In order to eliminate any suspicion of dual loyalty, it removed all references to Zion from its prayer-books and insisted that only the country in which Jews lived could be regarded as their legitimate homeland. This was particularly true in America where many of the new arrivals, Jews and non-Jews alike, believed that they had entered the Promised Land. To them, Reform was the most consistent Jewish religious expression of that new reality. Thus Max Lilienthal, an American rabbi, wrote:

> We Israelites of the present age do not dream any longer about the restoration of Palestine and the Messiah crowned with a diadem of earthly power and glory. America is our Palestine; here is our Zion and Jerusalem: Washington and the signers of the glorious Declaration of Independence – of universal human right, liberty and happiness – are our deliverers, and the time when their doctrines will be recognised and carried into effect is the time so hopefully foretold by our great prophets. When men will live together united in brotherly love, peace, justice and mutual benevolence, then the Messiah has come indeed, and the spirit of the Lord will have been revealed to all his creatures.[3]

Zionists regarded this as an illusion, and subsequent events vindicated them. The vision of the Reformers in America, Germany and elsewhere might have become reality, but it did not. Reform's hostility to Zionism had, in the logic of Emancipation and integration, some validity, but, in the light of contemporary history, it was misplaced and its effects less than fortunate. The Zionist suspicion of the West triumphed not because of Jewish obduracy but due to Gentile anti-Semitism, and today it is this suspicion that has become the norm

---

[3] Quoted in W. Gunther Plaut, *The Growth of Reform Judaism* (World Union for Progressive Judaism, New York, 1965), p. 145.

when it comes to Jewish survival strategy. The notion that the nations of the world would only respect the Jews if the Jews had a state of their own, or at least 'a national home' (as the earlier terminology had it) proved right. True, Western culture had much to offer and Zionist thinkers were influenced by it, but they believed that, to benefit from it, it had to be transplanted on to Jewish soil. To assimilate ourselves to it in the Diaspora – which by definition renounces Jewish sovereignty over Jewish destiny and expects the non-Jewish world to be master over it, sometimes benevolently, but often viciously – would spell the end of Jewry and Judaism.

After the Second World War the truth of this stance became apparent to most Jews. Zionism now became their most potent metaphor for hope. The establishment of the State of Israel, almost to the day three years after the defeat of Nazism, turned the hope into reality. The Jewish State became a haven for the homeless survivors from the European camps, from Arab lands, indeed from all over the world. To go and live in Israel and to be involved in some way, be it by giving money or time, with Israel is today in the minds of most Jews the most potent vehicle in the struggle for collective Jewish survival.

If anti-Semitism has brought together Jews of all persuasions into a negative coalition, Israel has united us for more positive reasons and, despite many differences about the politics of the Jewish State, the term 'Jewish solidarity' is almost invariably linked with support for Israel. When Israel is at risk – which, alas, is most of the time – all Jews feel threatened; the fear of anti-Semitism and the concern for the Jewish State become fused. When Israel flourishes – which, remarkably, is also almost all the time, despite her economic burdens and the military and political threats to her existence – Jews feel proud and secure wherever they live. Israel represents to us the living reality of rebirth and survival, the epitome of Fackenheim's commandment. Once again, our enemies have sensed this more accurately even than we ourselves, and they have labelled their anti-Semitism as anti-Zionism. Once they persecuted their contemporary Jews while professing their love for the people Jesus came from; today they express their love of a Judaism no longer in existence and which, to a very large extent, they themselves help to destroy while they villify their contemporaries who see in Israel and Zionism the most enduring guarantee for Jewish survival.

In this way, then, Fackenheim's formulation has become not only the central concern of Jewish theology today but, much more significantly, the guiding principle of contemporary Jewish life. Orthodoxy and Reform each deploy their own strategies in the Diaspora, but both find common ground in their affirmation of Zionism and Israel. *Within* the Jewish State they may be engaged in a bitter *Kulturkampf* about religious freedom, *outside* the Jewish State they quarrel over communal control, but they unite when issues *about* Israel are at stake. Israel binds the liberal to the fundamentalist, the atheist to the believer. All accept that it represents the tangible manifestation of the doctrine of survival as a supra-religious value transcending denominational differences.

The trauma of the Holocaust has produced an almost tribal response. Perhaps only psychologists can explain it; perhaps there is no explanation to be offered. But whether we view it positively or negatively, it is a fact of Jewish life and we must accept it as such if we are to make progress. To deny or belittle the fight for survival in today's Jewish world would be to be blind to reality. Only by recognizing its potency can we attempt to go beyond it in our search for purpose.

8

Vicarious Judaism

Although the quest for survival is a fact of Jewish life, and although you can hardly be involved in that life without participating in the struggle, it does not mean that it is possible to accept it uncritically. The sketch of the current strategies of survival is not offered as a mere *apologia* but as a prelude to a critical analysis. For it is my contention that the very thing that has made Jewish life possible after the catastrophe – the stress on survival as a religious category to which most other considerations are to be subservient – may also turn out to be a threat to the future of Judaism. A sure way of losing wars is to fail to adapt one's strategies in the face of changing circumstances. Fackenheim's dictum and the programme of action, which reflected the primacy of the commandment to survive, may have been appropriate in the first, and perhaps second, decade after the Holocaust, but it can never be more than an interim formula. Its continuous application has, as in the case of so many effective remedies, nasty side effects. Let us now look at some of them.

To start with, regular application of the survival formula reduces its effectiveness. Thus even those who wish to rouse Jews with the call for survival – often warning them of the continuous dual danger of intermarriage and anti-Semitism – find it increasingly difficult to command the necessary response. The danger has to increase, as it were, for the Jewish self-defence mechanism to come into operation. Occasionally Jewish leaders have been tempted to raise the temperature artificially to elicit expressions of Jewish loyalty, but people are becoming suspicious of all such efforts, and there is now a risk that they will remain indifferent even in moments of real danger, since they will not be able to distinguish between the genuine and the sham. Thus, for example, demonstrations against overtures to the Palestine Liberation Organization made by Western governments, or the intransigence of the Soviet Union in its treatment of Jews attract only a minority; they have all been there before and they are exhausted. Only a new factor, like increased evidence of French anti-Semitism, produces the required response, at least for a few weeks or months.

One of the most alarming effects of this exhaustion is the tendency to support causes and institutions in the hope that they will do the work for them. The stress on survival has produced a kind of vicarious Judaism; many Jews in the Diaspora are subscribers rather than members, expecting 'organized Jewry' to do the work of concerned Jews. In the United States this has resulted in the professionalization of the Jewish world. Synagogues and welfare organizations, campaigns and pressure groups, educational establishments and defence bodies to combat anti-Semitism and anti-Zionism, all tend to be run by professionals who not only do the administration but also determine the policies and raise the funds. We are seeing evidence of a growing alienation on the part of the individual Jew from his means of Jewish identity.

The three main streams in Jewish life – Orthodoxy, Reform and Zionism – have helped to create this alienation by concentrating so much on the issue of survival. Instead of seeking to evolve and articulate properly their respective approaches to Jewish life, they have sought to justify themselves by claiming to have the best formula for survival. As a result, they have often failed to keep the interest of their original adherents. To stimulate that interest, they have engaged professionals who, in turn, have further alienated the rank-and-file members. However, since the professionals have an interest in keeping the institutions that employ them going, they use their considerable skills to stifle every attempt to bring about change. The concerned laymen become disenchanted and withdraw and only the cynics and the less able remain at the helm, often as figure-heads and office holders of organizations they do not run and do not really understand. That is a major reason why Jewish leadership is frequently of such a low calibre.

Unfortunately, rabbis, too, have become professional *apparatchiks* dedicated to the task of keeping their jobs intact and enhancing their status. Traditionally, the rabbi's task is to teach and to decide in matters of law; until the Middle Ages he was not even supposed to be paid for his services. Today, however, he has become the executive director of his organization, which is often a synagogue, but an increasing number of rabbis have become professional civil servants running the other institutions that represent the Jewish communities in the Diaspora. If survival is the main plank of the platform of their religious ideology, it is not their ability to teach but their skills as administrators and politicians that is required. Administration has taken the place of ministration because the political aspirations of the collective have taken the place of the spiritual needs of the individual. This is true both in Orthodox and in non-Orthodox circles.

Authentic Orthodoxy seems only to be practised by a minority of extremists, who are Orthodox for no other reason than because they regard this as the only true expression of the will of God. For them, survival is the inescapable bi-product of their religious life. They adhere to the minutiae of Jewish law because the Torah has so commanded it; they have large families because they believe birth control to be sinful. In the process they may further Jewish survival, but what they are doing is not primarily for the sake of Jewish survival. They are doing the will of God, they believe, and because of this, God makes sure that they are being preserved.

By contrast, those who present Orthodoxy, in the first instance, as a method of Jewish survival, fail both Orthodoxy and the quest for survival. They contribute to the alienation and the type of vicarious Judaism which leads to apathy. They find 'right-wing' Orthodoxy philosophically untenable and do not abide by its tenets, neither do they practise its precepts. They belong to Orthodox communities – 'for the sake of Jewish survival' – but leave the actual practice to the professionals, i.e. the rabbis, who are the agents of their vicarious Judaism. In former years such communities used to have an inner circle of observant Jews who gave character and direction to the rest. Today, however, such activists find it increasingly unsatisfactory to be 'Jews for others' and tend to join small homogenous groups where everybody practises what is expected of him. As a result, mainstream Orthodoxy, epitomized in Britain by the United Synagogue and, elsewhere, by less well organized bodies, finds itself in a serious crisis of leadership and is characterized by an unholy alliance, perhaps a conspiracy, between professional and vicarious Jews. The latter expect from the former the kind of Judaism Papa and Mama used to make, not because they believe in it, but because they believe it to be conducive to Jewish survival.

The various manifestations of non-Orthodox Judaism on both sides of the Atlantic have attempted to step into the breach and offer an acceptable version of Judaism without making too many demands on its adherents. Nevertheless, Conservative, Reform and Liberal Judaism have each ended up offering yet another version of vicarious Judaism. Whereas mainstream Orthodoxy addresses itself to the nostalgic, the non-Orthodox movements tend to capture the indifferent. In theory, of course, they wish to speak to the cognitive minority that has rejected fundamentalism in favour of scientific truth and moral consistency. In practice, by projecting a less rigid image in the realm of observance, they seem to attract those who want the comforts of tradition without being burdened by the guilty conscience that may result from its unheeded demands. What goes under the name of honesty and integrity is often a mere camouflage for convenience. The professionals, myself included, seek to combat this officially, but perhaps subconsciously we encourage it. Both adherents of mainstream Orthodoxy and Reform choose to pay considerable sums of money to support synagogues and allied institutions of which they intend to take little advantage. In this way, for example, large and impressive buildings are being put up, which stand empty most of the year, but act as status symbols for those who only enjoy their Judaism vicariously. Rabbis, educators and administrators are being employed, and they submit budgets and devise programmes to justify their existence and consolidate their positions responding to the wants, but not to the real needs, of the people.

The most devastating effect of vicarious Judaism in its Reform version can be seen in its gradual but systematic withdrawal from the scene of social action. As Jews we have suffered much pain; our stress on survival is the result. Throughout history our suffering has also made us sensitive to the pain of others. In the post-emancipation epoch this expressed itself in a determined effort to diminish inequality, injustice and every other form of human suffering. In the last decades that effort has been less in evidence. That is partly due to the fact that recipients, often victims of anti-Semitic prejudice, have refused to take the Jewish hand that was being offered; the rebuff that concerned Jews received from Blacks in their efforts for civil rights in the United States is a telling illustration. But the Jewish withdrawal was also due to a growing propensity to leave the world to its own devices and to concentrate on Jewish survival, yet another manifestation of vicarious Judaism. Gentile, often Black, hostility and Jewish, even Reform, reluctance came thus to reflect and exemplify the uncanny collusion between anti-Semite and Jewish survivor which threatens to destroy the very fabric of Jewish teaching, in this instance its universalist emphasis on a just society.

What is true of the prevalent attitude to Jewish institutions in the Diaspora, often represented by the various religious movements, is in even larger measure true of the Diaspora's relationship to Israel. The Jewish State is the epitome of Jewish survival in our century; it probably also is the most popular vehicle for vicarious Judaism. Most of those who today go to live in Israel do not emigrate out of idealism, but because of lack of alternatives. This in no way diminishes the significance of their immigration or seeks to challenge Israel's right to exist – for to be able to provide a home and a future for Jews whom nobody else wants is an important part of the Zionist dream – but it does suggest that those who speak idealistically about the Jewish State very often live in the Diaspora and thus practise a particular form of vicarious Judaism, namely vicarious Zionism.

The old polemic definition of a Zionist as someone who collects money to employ another person who will persuade a third one to settle in Israel still holds true. The Zionist world can still be categorized in terms of fund raisers who, with the money they collect from people giving it as a token of their vicarious Judaism, employ officials who seek out individuals who will go and live in Israel. The alarming division between those who provide the funds, via the United Jewish Appeal in the United States and corresponding organizations in other countries, and the officials their money is used to employ in the Jewish Agency and the World Zionist

Organization is often overlooked, and, as a result, the real problem of Zionist bureaucracy is ignored. Also ignored is the barrier between the officials and the actual immigrants which leads to apparent lack of empathy on the part of the former and considerable disillusionment by the latter. The various attempts to put things right tend to fail, because those seeking to make the repairs are often part of the damage, i.e. they too are victims of the vicarious Judaism of which pro-Israel activities, or employment by Zionist agencies, are fashionable manifestations.

The Jewish State, in order to fulfil the expectations which virtually all Jews and many non-Jews have vested in it, must continue to be built up by idealists, i.e. by men and women who settle there because they see it as the fulfilment of the noblest ideals of Judaism. If Israel is to be primarily for those who have nowhere else to go, our expectations are not likely to be fulfilled. There is a great danger that this may be the case. We already know that the majority of Jews now coming out of the Soviet Union prefer to settle outside of Israel. It is reasonable to surmise that those who go to Israel do not always do so out of free choice but because of lack of any alternatives. Moreover, many Israelis, even those born and bred there, have left the country permanently and others would like to go, given the opportunity. Immigration from Western countries, where Jews have a free choice to go or to stay, is very small, despite the considerable efforts on the part of Zionist officials.

Most of those who work in the Zionist movement in the Diaspora, including the author of this book, may dream of going to live in the Jewish State, but take few practical steps to do so. We too are part of the vicarious Judaism syndrome. Those who do not have to go and live in Israel will work for it, visit it, speak of it with pride, defend it against attack and support every endeavour to secure its existence – because they might need it one day. In the meantime, they stay put in New York or London or Paris or even Johannesburg. They will speak with indignation about anti-Semitism – perhaps also because it may force them to leave their country of origin, as in the case of German Jewry when Hitler came to power – and with passion of the need for Jewish survival. But for the time being, at least, they are quite prepared to let the Israelis do the surviving for them, ignoring the fact that the Jewish State and its inhabitants have enough problems to safeguard their own survival without having to worry about the Diaspora. The Israelis also lack the necessary idealism to shoulder the burden of world Jewry's neurotic attitude to their faith and their land. They cannot be expected to be Jews for themselves and for others.

We often camouflage the fact that we expect Israel to do the surviving for us by speaking of interdependence. We say that Israel needs world Jewry as much as world Jewry needs Israel, and there is, of course, much truth in this. But there is no evidence that the individual Israeli seeks to express his Judaism with much consideration for Jewish life in the Diaspora, thus contrasting the Diaspora mentality, which very often looks to Israel to lead the Jewish life it is incapable, or unwilling to lead by itself. When Israelis are disappointed in world Jewry it is not because the latter is not sufficiently observant or knowledgeable – that is not expected – but because it has not yet settled in the land of our fathers. Diaspora Jews, by contrast, tend to be disappointed with Israelis that they do not practise the Judaism they, the Jews from outside, themsleves neglect or ignore. Love of Israel, Zionism as a whole, thus often becomes a manifestation of vicarious Judaism, as does Orthodoxy and Reform.

The quest for survival, in itself legitimate, noble and necessary has led many Jews into expecting others to do the surviving for them. The three main streams, have colluded with this expectation, because the religious essence of Judaism, which is concerned about the life of the individual before the survival of the collective, has been weakened. The weakening of the religious centre manifests itself as growing secularization.

9

Secularization

Vicarious Judaism is a by-product of the current emphasis on collective survival in place of personal salvation. As long as institutions such as the synagogue function, the individual Jew does not feel responsible for Jewish survival. He may be aware that schools and synagogues, organizations and societies are made up of people, individuals whose efforts are required to make the institutions flourish, but in practice he works on the assumption that someone else will actually do the work. If necessary, he will pay for it, but he does not really wish to be bothered. That is how a class of professional Jews – rabbis, administrators, fund-raisers and social workers – has emerged and come to dominate contemporary Jewish life.

The power and relative success of such professionals has in turn been possible because of the other major force that has operated in contemporary Judaism: secularization. In theory, there is no room for secularization in the Jewish scheme of things. The Bible does not even have a word for 'religion' [1] and Jewish tradition has never attempted to distinguish between the 'religious' and the 'secular' but regarded all aspects of human existence as God's domain and thus the concern of religion. Secularization is the product of Christian bifurcation [2] which distinguishes between the Church and the world, the spirit and the flesh. Because Christianity does not see faith as an integral part of life, but something outside it, to be imposed

---

[1] The modern Hebrew word *dat* is a Perisian loan-word which really means 'law'. It is used in Israel today and reflects Orthodoxy's legalistic concept of the Jewish religion. To be *dati* is to be 'religious'; the opposite is *chiloni* 'secular'. Both terms are linguistic inventions that lack real basis in the sources, but they do describe a reality that cannot be ignored.

[2] See Monford Harris, 'The Bifurcated Life' in *Judaism*, viii (1959), p. 99 ff.

on it almost by supernatural endeavour, when life and faith were separated, secularization – existence without God – became a reality. Many modernist doctrines can be viewed as secularized religions which have replaced the conventional ones and which threaten Christianity precisely because, in so many ways, they are similar to it and yet, paradoxically, diametrically opposed to it at the same time. The relationship of Marxism – secularized Christianity in which the proletariat has become the new priesthood and the rigid and immutable laws of economics the new dogmatic theology – to Christianity is a case in point.

Christian theologians are, of course, very critical of the secularizing process, both outside the Church and within it. Thus the many versions of Bonhoeffer's 'religionless Christianity', which characterized the theological climate of the 1960s and 1970s have not gone unchallenged. Critics have repeatedly accused the contemporary Church of politicizing and secularizing Christianity in its endeavours to be 'relevant' in the modern age. A book on contemporary Judaism is not the proper forum for an analysis of the debate within Christianity. The reference in this context is primarily to indicate that the critique is also applicable to the Jewish condition.

The notion that man has 'come of age' is often used to legitimize secularization. Peter L. Berger, the sociologist, castigates the religious exponents of our time for defending religion with weapons prepared by the enemies of religion.[3] Contemporary Jewish thought is no less guilty of this than Christian theology. Jewish spokesmen frequently seek to justify Judaism in terms of other disciplines and ideologies, thus deluding themselves that they are contributing to the fight for Jewish survival. True, such a secularist apologetic does appeal to the masses, but it is questionable whether it contributes to the continuity and vitality of Judaism. Instead, it seems to be the victim of the forces of secularism which, in the long run, see it as their aim to destroy conventional religion. Theology becomes bureaucracy; rabbis and teachers become officials, professional Jews.

In theory, Judaism need not have been affected by all that, since, as it were, secularism was already contained in the

3 See Peter L. Berger, *A Rumour of Angels*, (Penguin 1971).

Jewish religion. In practice, of course, it turned out very differently and Judaism, too, became secularized. Marxism itself came to have an effect on Jewish thought and Jewish life; it was the driving force behind the pioneering spirit of most of the early settlers in Palestine. The original motivation to settle in the land of our fathers may have been religious, for the yearning for Zion was central in the liturgy of Judaism and in the thought of every Jew, but the actual execution was often done by men and women who had rejected the Jewish religion in favour of secular Marxism. Zionism, despite its religious foundations, has become a largely secular movement.

Significantly, Zionism in its secular version, both before the establishment of the State of Israel and since, has always supported an unenlightened Orthodox religious establishment. It is as if the majority of the population always needed synagogues in which they would never set foot, and religious officials they would only call on for so-called 'life-cycle events', i.e. circumcision, perhaps *Barmitsvah* (although in Israel that is often celebrated without the benefit of clergy and outside of the synagogue), but not for any real spiritual guidance. Secular Israelis have a need, so it seems, to maintain religious institutions which will keep the faith on their behalf but, at the same time, by the extremist nature of these institutions, make sure that the majority of Israelis have nothing to do with them. In this way the dominant religion of the Jewish State has become institutionalized vicarious Judaism.

The situation is not very different in the Diaspora. In countries where Christian institutions belong to the 'establishment', as in Britain, or when religious affiliation is a mark of bourgeois respectability, as in the United States, the Jews have adapted their own heritage to imitate the dominant culture. The more secular society becomes, the greater is the need for religious institutions that are remote from life and which do not engage the individual.

That is why, both in Israel and in the Diaspora, Orthodoxy is surprisingly dominant, especially the kind of religious legalism which demands conformity in public, but does not seek to enforce observance on the individual in private. In this way it can pretend to speak for a solidly Orthodox community. It is, therefore, not surprising that neither the Orthodox Chief Rabbinate in Israel nor that in Britain have spoken out against the creeping secularization among Jews, for it is the secularization that makes for vicarious religion which favours their kind of Orthodoxy. The collusion between the indifferent majority and the few professionals has deep roots and representatives in high places.

The ire of Orthodox spokesmen has, instead, been directed against non-Orthodox religious manifestations of Judaism, for it is the latter that seek to challenge secularism and oppose vicarious Judaism. If they succeed, the need for an Orthodox establishment will diminish. The chances of success for these non-Orthodox groupings are, however, very small, because the secularists do not really want them. Somehow, it is easier for an avowed non-believer to know why he stays away from an Orthodox synagogue than from a Reform one. And, as suggested earlier, the success in the Diaspora of non-Orthodox Judaism is largely due to the fact that it had allowed itself to be used for secular purposes. Reform Judaism in America, for example, is in many ways the establishment religion, to which the rich and the respectable and the indifferent sub- scribe, but in which they do not really participate. In many ways it seeks to serve the middle-class needs of its distant supporters, instead of the spiritual needs of its committed members. The most popular courses in the adult education programme of many a congregation are not those on Jewish sources, Jewish observance or current Jewish thought, but on 'Kitchen-Spanish' to enable conversation with the Mexican maids that one so often finds in Californian Jewish house- holds, or on Yoga, not on account of a fascination with Eastern religions but because of a significantly secularist preoccupa- tion with health and appearance.

The most common manifestation of secularized religion today is, of course, the substitution of therapy for religion. In the words of Christopher Lasch: 'The contemporary climate is therapeutic, not religious. People today hunger not for personal salvation, . . . but for the feeling, the momentary illusion, of personal well-being, health, and psychic securi- ty.' [4] That is why doctors, psychiatrists and social workers so often have had to assume the traditional role of priests and rabbis, and that is why priests and rabbis, in an effort to stay

[4] Christopher Lasch, *The Culture of Narcissism* (Abacus 1980), p. 33.

in the race, take upon themselves the role of counsellors and therapists. As a result, the spiritual needs of congregants are being ignored or identified only as neuroses. The secularization process has thus transformed the life of many communities; people no longer come together in them to help and support each other but use the 'experts' these communities provide for specific 'services', not of the divine but of the social variety.

In the Diaspora, every form of religious establishment is losing ground. This is true of 'mainstream' Orthodoxy in Britain as it is of 'classical' Reform in America. For Diaspora Jewry has found a new outlet for its vicarious Judaism: the State of Israel. In the minds of many, the Jewish State has become the modern secular equivalent of the medieval Church, which it is sinful to criticize but not necessary to believe in. The fact that the State of Israel, like the religion of Israel, is central to Judaism and to Jewish survival gives substance to the fear that by criticizing it we are offering ammunition to the enemies that wish to destroy us. This rational consideration, however, is often coupled with the irrational need on the part of the secularist to have an idol which he can worship vicariously, in this case by giving money to Israel and perhaps occasionally visiting the country – which almost invariably is an exhilarating experience for Jew and non-Jew alike – to unveil a plaque, literally or metaphorically, which offers tangible evidence of his efforts and achievements.

The secular–religious character of the State of Israel is tellingly reflected in the Kol Nidre Appeal, which takes place in many synagogues. Yom Kippur, the Day of Atonement, is the holiest day in the Jewish year. The service on the eve of Yom Kippur is called Kol Nidre, after the opening words of a prayer which introduces that service. Many Jews, in some communities the majority, are in synagogue that night. That is why the Joint Israel Appeal in Britain, and corresponding agencies in other countries, have persuaded the rabbis and lay leaders of communities to allow an appeal for funds for Israel on that occasion. There is no notion of 'filthy lucre' in Jewish tradition and to appeal for charity in the High Holyday period, of which the Day of Atonement is the climax, is by no means uncommon. But to make an appeal from the pulpit a central feature of the Kol Nidre service is new and indicative of the secularizing tendency in contemporary Jewry. Conventional religion has here been combined with nationalist aspirations and both have been used as a channel for the individual Jew's need to express himself vicariously yet tangibly: he pledges a sum of money, well within his means (so that no real sacrifice is involved), by neatly fixing a piece of string in an appropriate hole on a card already bearing his name and displayed on his seat (thus not violating the law against writing on this Sabbath of Sabbaths).

The need for Jews to give of their worldly goods for the support of their brothers and sisters in the Jewish State is not questioned here. Financial support for Israel by Diaspora Jewry is crucial, and I myself am actively involved in campaigning for such funds. Nevertheless, the use of the most sacred occasion in the Jewish calendar for such campaigning is characteristic of the mood in contemporary Jewry. The quest for survival has identified sanctity with collecting money for Israel. Secularization has triumphed once again.

Although we cannot but view the phenomenon of the Kol Nidre Appeal critically, we must also understand its background. The pain that the Jewish people has carried through the ages, and experienced with particular severity in our century, has been made bearable through the establishment of the State of Israel. To support its continued existence is, therefore, a kind of religious obligation for every Jew. It is also a practical expression of the desire to alleviate the pain of others: significantly, the Kol Nidre Appeal is often made on behalf of the poor and the deprived inhabitants of the Jewish State. In this way support for Israel is also the Jewish equivalent of commitment to the Third World. That is its positive dimension. But, at the same time, this attempt to alleviate pain threatens to deprive Judaism of its religious dimension and Jewish history of its transcendent thrust. The duty to alleviate pain is paramount, but it will have to be expressed in more appropriate ways to be effective.

10

The Language of Satan

The purpose of those who seek to make out of secularism a tool for Jewish survival, and out of the State of Israel a Jewish Church, is a noble one. The determination not to give Hitler a posthumous victory dominates contemporary Jewish life. Nothing that is being written on these pages is to minimize that determination, or to devalue the enterprise. The critique is directed against the method in the conviction that to fight merely for survival is to endanger survival; only when survival is the necessary prerequisite for purpose can it be realized, and much of the purpose achieved. That purpose is to do God's work. Fackenheim's call not to give Hitler his victory may have shaped modern Jewish life, but we must now consider the gruesome prospect that the victory gained over Hitler's ghost may turn out to be a Pyrrhic one. The stress on our survival and the secularization that has been elevated to the level of religion in the quest for survival, appears to have banished God from Jewish consciousness and replaced Him, in secular-humanist fashion, with the Jewish People. Christian theologians have spoken of the death of God; their Jewish counterparts should perhaps speak of the banishment of God, a concept to which there are many references in the sources of Judaism. But whereas these sources normally imply that it is the machinations of the Gentiles against His People that have put God into exile, the irony of the present condition is that it is the quest for the continuation of the People that seems to have doomed God to oblivion.

The faith of Israel rests on three pillars: trust in God; belief in the authenticity and validity of His will as revealed in the Torah; and the conviction that the Jewish People has been given the task to make His will, and thereby His Presence, known to the world and manifest in its own actions and lifestyle. Judaism becomes dangerously lop-sided and disturbed when it rests on only one or two of these pillars. It would be too simplistic a view to suggest, as has been done sometimes, that Orthodoxy rests primarily on Torah, Reform on God and Zionism on People, because labels are not always relevant in our context. However, there is some validity in the contention that all modernist movements in Judaism have come to lean too much on the pillar People and too little on the pillar God, thus putting themselves in a precarious situation. I have sought the cause of this distinction in the secularization process and attempted to identify its principal manifestation in the universal quest for survival. Later in this volume I will try to suggest a formula of restoration; at this stage I am only setting out to define the problem and to point to the direction of a possible solution: a re-emphasis of trust in God.

If such trust is to us what Jewish tradition teaches that it is – the trust of the Biblical Isaac in his father, and the trust of the father in his God, the Heavenly Father, when (as *Genesis* 22 tells it) both father and son ascend Mount Moriah – then it must follow that God, not the Jewish People, will ultimately decide whether that people is to survive or not. In this scheme of things, then, survival ceases to be a human preoccupation and becomes a divine responsibility. Man's role is to do God's will to the best of his ability, as laid down in His Torah and understood by tradition through the ages. It is not man's task to do God's work for Him.

Arthur Koestler's description of free will and determinism offers us something of a model of the proper relationship between faith and survival when he writes that 'all our bodily and mental skills are governed by *fixed rules* and more or less *flexible strategies*'.[1]

God who revealed Himself to Abraham is the fixed rule, the struggle for Jewish survival a flexible strategy. When the strategy becomes the rule, secularization has taken place. There is much to suggest that that is precisely what has been happening in Jewish life and thought in our times. We have come to worship the strategy – the Jewish People; the Jewish State; survival – and thus set aside the fixed rule: God and

[1] Arthur Koestler, *Janus – A Summing Up* (Hutchinson 1978), p. 236.

His Torah. In Biblical times this was known as idolatry. It may still have to be described thus.

A Jewish tale has it that, on his way to Mount Moriah, Abraham met Satan who, quite logically, told him that if he, Abraham, went ahead and offered up his son, it would be the end of the Jewish people, since Isaac was his only legitimate heir. To which Abraham replied: 'My task is to do God's will and to obey Him; His is the problem of Jewish survival.'

It is understandable why, after the Holocaust and in the light of the dual threat of anti-Semitism and assimilation, the contemporary Jew finds it so difficult to share his ancestor's trust. Satan's argument makes more sense to him. But, however difficult it may seem, he must also be made to realize that all the stress on survival may, in the long run, turn out to be the language of Satan. If that happens, the ability to feel pain will have been trivialized and the purpose of Jewish existence lost. In the words of Gershom Scholem:

> Beyond physical survival in extreme situations, the import-
> ance of which we have all come to recognize, and in the
> very actualization of which great human and socially dy-
> namic forces manifest themselves, the question will be
> always put precisely – and with good reason *to us* whether
> we will have more to offer to our people than this survival.[2]

---

[2] Gershom Scholem, *On Jews and Judaism in Crisis* (Schocken, New York, 1976), p. 258.

III

THE CHALLENGE OF RADICALISM

Testimony as a Call to Repentance

> Every age brings its own unique problems, but somehow every age also brings its solutions. What is important, however, is that we should not rely on miracles.
>
> Emanuel Rackman[1]

---

[1] Emanuel Rackman, 'A Happy New Year?' *The Jewish Chronicle*, 5 September 1980, p. 50.

11

The Need for Prophecy

In order to face up to Satan and to meet his argument, a radically new approach to Jewish existence is needed. For only a reconsideration of the present fashion in Jewish thought will enable us to be true to our heritage. The intention is not to deny the fact that Judaism is impossible without Jews, i.e. that peoplehood is central to the Jewish scheme of things, but, rather, to affirm that Judaism is pointless without God, i.e. that only through the affirmation of our purpose does the continued existence of the Jewish people make sense. Only a radical stance will enable us to recognize that to clamour for survival, while ignoring other considerations, is, in the last resort, to speak with the voice of Satan.

It is a painful recognition, because the experience of Jewish suffering under the Nazis, and the threat to Jewish life in Israel from the Arabs and their friends, has put all Jews in the grip of a trauma which makes it almost impossible to dissent from the general stress on survival without being regarded as a renegade. Any Jewish spokesman who dares to be critical of the way the Holocaust is used in Jewish polemics, or who makes political statements to the effect that intransigence towards Arabs is not the best way of securing Jewish survival, runs the risk of being vilified. The matter is further complicated by the fact that such vilification is not without justification, for any discordant voice, however constructive, is almost invariably exploited by the enemies of Jews and of Israel who seek to offer 'evidence' to the effect that the six million never died and that the Jewish State is based on a racist ideology. As a result, it is very difficult, if not impossible, to make responsible statements about contemporary Jewish life without becoming a tool in the hands of those who seek to annihilate us.

And yet, despite the dangers, Satan has to be unmasked and his words exposed for what they are. This becomes especially necessary when the trauma of the Holocaust is used as a justification for Israeli extremist policies. The insolence and falsity behind such a link has been forcefully expressed by Cordelia Edvardson, a journalist living in Israel:

> It seems like sacrilege to me when Mr Begin and his followers are bolstering their political views, which they of course are entitled to hold, with reference to my and others' experiences in the Holocaust. The Holocaust is not, was not, and can never be used as an argument for the Jewish people's right to rule over another people, i.e. one million Arabs on the West Bank and in Gaza. Even I am prepared to say: 'NEVER AGAIN'. But my experience has taught me that you can destroy a people physically, but you also can destroy it spiritually.

Edvardson then goes on to list some examples of how the defence of physical continuity reflects a dangerous kind of spiritual destruction and concludes:

> What we need now is exactly the 'voice of reason' so we may be able to choose between good and evil, and we, and others with us, may live . . . I am confident that the majority of my people, the Jewish people, will soon listen again to the voice of reason.[1]

What is described above as 'the "voice of reason" so that we may be able to choose between good and evil' can be identified as the voice of Prophecy, as understood in our tradition. Throughout the Bible, the Prophets seek to assess history, be it recent or ancient, as well as contemporary politics, not from the perspective of expediency and popular mythology, but from God's perspective. They see themselves not as the hired spokesmen of potentates – like Balaam – but as the true spokesmen of God and, therefore, prepared to articulate a higher reason, whether it is popular or not, in order to make it possible for the people to make the right choice.

[1] Cordelia Edvardson, 'A Survivor's Voice' in *The Jewish Quarterly* London, xxviii, 1 (102) (Spring 1980), p. 65.

See, I set before you this day life and prosperity, death and adversity. For I command you this day, to love the Lord your God, to walk in His ways, and to keep His commandments, His laws, and His rules, that you may thrive and increase, and that the Lord your God may bless you in the land which you are about to invade and occupy . . . I call heaven and earth to witness against you this day: I have put before you life and death, blessing and curse. Choose life – if you and your offspring would live – by loving the Lord your God, heeding His commands, and holding fast to Him. For thereby you shall have life and shall long endure upon the soil that the Lord your God swore to Abraham, Isaac and Jacob to give to them. (*Deuteronomy* 30:15–16, 19–20).

The choice, in our context, is between the voice of Satan and the call of God. In our times, as in earlier ages, it is only the Prophetic stance that can expose the former for what it is and open our ears to the latter. Our concern is not with politics in the narrow sense of the word, i.e. the attitude of the Israeli government to this or that issue, but with the much wider question of the mood of contemporary Jewry. We must seek to address ourselves to the general theme of the quest for survival, as it has become articulated after the Holocaust, and in the wake of the establishment of the State of Israel, in relation to the teachings of Judaism. And we must attempt this from the perspective of Biblical Prophecy, since that is the most stable and consistent framework for Jewish value judgment.

It is not an easy task. Not only because the use of Prophecy in polemics is an old and often abused device, but also because to adopt a Prophetic stance some 2,500 years after the time of the last Biblical Prophet is both anachronistic and arrogant. After the destruction of the Second Temple, the Rabbis taught, the gift of Prophecy was taken from the Sages and given to fools. Every attempt to invoke Prophecy and to speak in the manner of the Biblical Prophets opens itself to that accusation.

The three main manifestations of contemporary Judaism, referred to in this book repeatedly as Orthodoxy, Reform and Zionism, each illustrate the abuse of Prophecy in the service of their respective sectarian claims. All three insist that *they* are the true heirs of the Biblical Prophets, despite the fact that, at closer examination, it appears that they very often espouse teachings which were anathema to the Prophets. One of the ways in which the modern Jew is being mystified is that the ideology to which he subscribes claims to be the authentic exponent of traditions which, when examined through the sources, seem to be saying the opposite. His teachers, often with a vested interest in the ideology they represent, have, therefore, reasons for keeping him ignorant and confused, unless he is prepared to echo their prejudices. Much of the so-called crisis in Jewish education is linked with the doctrinaire nature of the systems under which it is provided. The only way of gaining objectivity is through pure scholarship, but that requires so much expertize and detailed knowledge that only the select few can attain it, and even then only in a very limited area, rarely across the whole spectrum of Jewish tradition. The notion of holy study accessible to the interested and committed layman has largely disappeared as a result of ideological and political superstructures. The contemporary layman is being deliberately mystified – and then castigated for his ignorance. In this way the power of the professional Jews remains intact. Neither the *shiur*, the traditional study session in the Orthodox *shool*, where people gather to study and to pray, nor the adult education group in the Reform Synagogue, nor the lecture series in the Zionist society, not even the course organized by some institution in Israel, enable the participant to have a reasonably accurate picture of what his tradition really has to say. It is true, of course, that no sources can be read without interpretation – there is, as it were, no Written Teaching without Oral Teaching – but when that interpretation is consistently being distorted, there is cause for alarm.

The distortion can be easily recognized in the conventional approach of the three streams in today's Judaism. Thus modern Orthodoxy has tended to identify the principles of Prophetic Judaism with the practices embodied in the *Halacha* (Jewish Law), and so put too much emphasis on Torah at the expense of God and Israel. True, Pharisaic Judaism saw itself as the carrier of Prophetic ideals which it sought to translate into practical action, but there is a far cry from the openness and richness of the Judaism of the Mishna, the Midrash and the Talmud to the relative poverty and uniformity of the Judaism of the Codes and their modern interpreters and custodians. The Jew who loves the warmth of his Orthodox Synagogue is nevertheless mystified by the coldness and rigidity of the legalism on which it is based. He has to rely on the ingenuity and public relations ability of his rabbi, his professional Jew, to persuade him that behind the cold letter of the law there is a warm spirit that speaks in the name of God and for the good of His people. If he ceases to argue, it is not necessarily because he is convinced but because he knows that in the Orthodox scheme of things, as in every totalitarian system, to show dissent is to be labelled ignorant and feeble-minded.

Reform came into being as a reaction against the cold law, but brought little warmth in its place and, again, tended to mystify many of its adherents. Its lofty claims of ethical monotheism, based on the words of the Prophets, set out to assert the primacy of God over both Torah and Israel, but the God it described had more similarities with the Kantian abstraction, 'the categorical imperative', than with the living Reality that revealed Itself to Abraham, Isaac and Jacob. Reform anti-legalism soon turned into a dogma and the fact that the Prophets were only critical of the Priestly abuse of the law, not of the law as such, was conveniently ignored, especially since the bulk of Christian antinomian (and often anti-Semitic) Bible scholarship supported such an interpretation. The Jew who came to the Reform synagogue in search of the passion that permeated Prophetic writings, read and quoted in that synagogue, encountered only decorum and decency, of which he approved but which did not move him to perceive God in 'the still small voice'.

Zionism distorted the message of the Biblical Prophets by insisting that it could only come into its own on the land where it was spoken. In this way Israel could be limited to a State and God reduced to a political argument, with Torah as a mere guidebook in geography. Prophetic Judaism could thus be used as a tool in the process of politicization and secularization, and since the State was, after the Holocaust, legitimately recognized as an essential tool in the struggle for survival, the message of the Prophets could be identified with it. The fact that their concern was wider than the State could be conveniently ignored. Jeremiah's letter to the exiles in Babylonia – 'build houses and live in them, plant gardens and eat their fruit . . . and seek the welfare of the city to which I have exiled you and pray to the Lord in its behalf; for in its prosperity you shall prosper' (*Jeremiah* 29:5 and 7) – embraces a vision larger than any single piece of land, and his hope for Israel is not confined to one specific country.

Not that the three modernist movements in Judaism were entirely wrong in their perception of Prophetic Judaism. They all contain elements of the teachings of the Prophets. However, none of them can claim to be *the* authentic exponent of such teachings, for they each came to stress one aspect at the expense of others in order to legitimize their respective ideologies. The picture of Judaism that we seek to present here is a complex one, not without tensions and contradictions, and, in order to paint it more adequately, we must abandon institutional allegiances and denominational slogans in an effort to understand the Prophets afresh and, without preconceived ideas, seek to discover ways of following in their footsteps. For our endeavour is to go behind the immediate task of surviving in order to discover our true purpose as the Children of Israel.

In this connection we ought to make it clear that we do not see Prophets as people who made prognostications about the future. They were, in that often quoted phrase, not *foretellers* but *forthtellers*. They did not tell their contemporaries what *will* happen, but what *ought to* happen. They are, therefore, not to be confused with the futurologists of our time. Our stress on the primacy of Prophetic Judaism must not be seen as an attempt to predict the future of Judaism. It is the moral content of the message, not the clairvoyant capacity of the messenger, that makes for true Prophecy. And it always contains the dimension of hope: man *can* change his ways and, therefore, alter the course of events. That is why the response to Prophecy is moral action, never helpless resignation, which is what many tend to feel when reading futurologists' predictions.

Biblical Prophets and modern futurologists reflect a fundamental difference between hope and calculation. The former is based both on commitment to morality and faith in

God, and will be discussed at the end of this book; the latter depends on projections of present conditions as seen by statisticians and sociologists. Prophetic hope gives us the confidence to look at long-term aims and not only at short-term strategies, at purpose and not only at survival. The calculations of the futurologists, by contrast, easily evoke in us unjustified anxiety about Jewish survival and move us to engage in different Jewish forms of doom watching. Trust in God enables us to refute Satan's argument the way Abraham did; belief in statistics makes us Satan's victims. We become such victims when we secularize our Judaism and become blind to the higher purpose of Jewish existence, which permeates Prophetic Judaism.

Orthodoxy, Reform and Zionism have in this sense become the victims of futurology – despite their protestations about their allegiance to the Hebrew Prophets – because they have each implied that the other movements' perception of Judaism is doomed to failure and bound to lead to self-annihilation. Thus mainstream Orthodoxy regards Reform as a short stop-over on the way to total assimilation, and extreme Orthodoxy sees Zionism as the most potent force which prevents the advent of the Messiah. Reform, in turn, often looks at Orthodoxy as the movement that makes progress impossible and thus a Jewish future unlikely and, for a long time, it has regarded Zionism as a betrayal of Judaism because of its lack of interest in the purely 'religious'. Zionism, finally, has tended to view both the other movements as forces that make for Jewish extinction because they imply a belief in the Diaspora. In their critique of each other, they have applied the tools of futurologists who often see themselves as the only possessors of the truth which entitles them to dismiss all alternatives. Such analyses tend to become self-fulfilling 'prophecies'. Our fear today ought to be that all the three movements in contemporary Judaism are right about each other and wrong about themselves.

True Prophetic Judaism, with its built-in hope, is, by contrast, inclusive; the Hebrew word for hope, tikva, comes from a root that means 'to gather'. Hope affirms all that reflects faith and trust and acts as a tool of God's will; it denounces all that stands in the way, irrespective of institutional affiliation. It is this kind of hope that makes for Messianic vision, which views the present not as something fixed out of which the future can be extrapolated, but as the necessary preparation for what will be.

Whereas the model of futurologists is the present, the model of Prophets is the past, especially the ancient Kingdom of David. The Messiah is the 'anointed King', a descendant of the Davidic dynasty. But it is not an escape into the past. When the people will live by God's teachings, as revealed in both Scripture and interpretation, past, present and future will merge into eternity. By striving for this, history will be hallowed, the present will gain meaning and the future will be assured. All alternatives make this impossible and, therefore, have to be exposed for what they are: manifestations of idolatry.

Our analysis of contemporary Judaism brings us to the conclusion that only a return to an authentically Prophetic approach to Jewish existence, the approach reflected in Scripture and manifest in Jewish Messianic aspirations throughout the ages, will enable us to make sense out of our history, improve things as we find them today and work towards a better future. However, before we can attempt a more detailed description of this modern adaptation of Prophetic Judaism, we must endeavour to understand yet another of its characteristic features: its radicalism.

12

A Radical Critique

The message of hope usually comes at the end of the Prophet's speech. The bulk of his message – often described as *massa*, 'bulk' or 'burden' – consists of a radical critique of the world around him. The critical appraisal of the three movements in modern Judaism offered here should be viewed in this way. Not that it makes any Prophetic claims for itself, but it attempts to view contemporary Jewish life from the same perspective as the Prophets viewed events and movements in their days. It is a radical perspective.

The nature of Prophetic radicalism and its relevance for today can also be perceived in contemporary Christian theology, which sees radicalism not only as a political category, but also as an attitude of mind. It is often represented as built-in challenge to any establishment, institution, or orthodoxy. Ideological commitment or institutional allegiance have to be disregarded, therefore, for the sake of truth. But the critique to which this Prophetic-radical stance leads is the critique of an insider. The radical is a man who, as the word itself suggests, goes to the roots of *his own* tradition. To do that he must love that tradition: he must – as the Biblical Prophet did – weep over Jerusalem, even when he has to pronounce its doom. The radical critique of contemporary Judaism should, ideally, be of this kind.

'It is an impressive sign of religious vitality that religious radicalism should have reappeared in authentically twentieth-century Jewish and Christian thought,' writes Fackenheim.[1] It is not the vitality of heretics, for the radical's roots must go deep enough to provide the security from which

[1] Emil L. Fackenheim, *The Jewish Return into History* (Schocken, New York, 1978), p. 8.

to question, even to the fundamentals. No one can be a radical who is uncertain of his tenure. Those who today appear to defend their own ideological points of reference, right or wrong, and refuse to question any aspect of their faith or any manifestation of Jewish statehood or Israeli government policy may, in fact, be displaying a fundamental insecurity, or uncertainty of tenure, which is camouflaged through excessive zeal. It is doubtful whether, in the long run, Judaism, or even their particular cause, is served by their stance. It may be understandable in the face of the many enemies that surround us Jews and seek to exploit our constructive self-criticism for their destructive aims, but it is also possible that, to some extent at least, it is our insecurity that helps to feed the myth of their enmity thus absolving us from showing courage of the type that Prophets displayed.

To express a desire to emulate the Hebrew Prophets is embarrassing, because it is in the nature of religious institutions to inculcate in their adherents a sense of modesty that borders on self-denigration. All three movements in contemporary Judaism are guilty of this, Orthodoxy by its very nature more so than the others. To claim courage in the tradition of Biblical Prophets is viewed, in this scheme of things, as *hubris*, or at least *chutspa*. The myth that prevents us from acting critically and responsibly has it that contemporaries are but dwarfs, compared to the giants of long ago. The fact that even if we are dwarfs, we still stand on the shoulders of the giants of the past is ignored. So is the Rabbinic dictum that 'Jephta in his generation was as great as Samuel was in his'.[2] It is not suggested that, had the two men lived at the same time, their qualities would have been comparable, but nevertheless each was of the same importance in their time. Even if we are not Samuels but Jephtas, we still have a duty to act as if we were the greatest, for there is nobody else. Religious leaders, be they Jews or Christians or Muslims, often choose to shun responsibility by displaying modest piety and reverence for the past. By elevating our predecessors beyond reach or emulation we appear to display humility. In reality, however, we may be merely avoiding responsibility.

[2] Bab. Talmud, *Rosh Hashanah* 25b.

A further reason for such escape of responsibility may be due to the fact that our leaders lack passion. The age of scientific detachment has imposed on religious teachers a need to imitate detached scholars in order to gain respectability. The Biblical Prophets put no such restraints on themselves. They were men of passion, rooted in their deep faith. They were insiders who dared to question, even to mock themselves and others in the service of God. And yet, they were not marginal figures who had 'freaked out', but teachers of whom the masses may have disapproved but whom they could not ignore. King Zedekiah may have decided that Jeremiah had to be put in prison, but that did not prevent the monarch from calling the Prophet out at night to consult him on matters of state.[3] In the quest for acceptability and popularity the religious leaders of today rarely find themselves in such a dialectical relationship to political power. As a result, they may not be vilified, but they are being ignored. Much of the *malaise* of Jewish life today is the result of the timidity of the leaders and the indifference of the led.

One of the most important insights into the nature of Prophecy that A. J. Heschel has taught concerns Prophetic pathos, which he puts in contrast to power:

> In the interpretation of religion it is generally assumed that God is, above all, 'the name for some experience of power'. That power is mysterious, *ne plus ultra*. Such interpretation, valid as it may be for the understanding of other types of religion, hardly applies to the Prophets. Here the reality of the divine is sensed as pathos rather than as power, and the most exalted idea applied to God is not infinite wisdom, infinite power, but infinite concern. He who does not live on others, cares for others.[4]

Tracing the notion of the detachment of the divine from human affairs from Greek philosophy until modern times – and the effect of that approach on Jewish thought in the Middle Ages – Heschel juxtaposes the Biblical idea of pathos with the Stoic doctrine of apathy: 'The ideal state of the Stoic sage is apathy, the ideal state of the Prophet is sympathy. The

---

[3] *Jeremiah* 38:14 ff.
[4] A. J. Heschel, *The Prophets* (JPSA, Philadelphia, 1962), p. 241.

Greeks attributed to the gods the state of happiness and serenity; the Prophets thought of God's relation to the world as one of concern and compassion.' [5] There is no doubt, however, as to which approach Heschel advocates:

> Impressive as is the thought that God is too sublime to be affected by events on this insignificant planet, it stems from a line of reasoning about a God derived from abstraction. A God of abstraction is a high and mighty First Cause, which, dwelling in the lonely splendour of eternity, will never be open to human prayer; and to be affected by anything which it has itself caused to come into being would be beneath the dignity of an abstract God. This is a dogmatic sort of dignity, insisting upon pride rather than love, upon decorum rather than mercy.
>
> In contrast with the *primum movens immobile*, the God of the Prophets cares for His creatures, and His thoughts are about the world. He is involved in human history and is affected by human acts. It is a paradox beyond compare that the Eternal God is concerned with what is happening in time. [6]

When we now speak of the need for Prophecy it is such passion that we have in mind. Of course, despite our insistence that we have to take responsibility for our religious life, we do not presume to make claims of direct divine communication. This is not a disguised attempt to restate the old liberal doctrine of 'progressive revelation', implying that God speaks to all men at all times. There is no 'thus says the Lord' at the end of this book. Nevertheless it is legitimate to seek the inspiration that came from the passion and the faith that permeated the lives of the Biblical Prophets in an endeavour to challenge, perhaps even to change a little, the accepted norms of Jewish life. It is this search that brings us to our radical critique.

It has to be said again that it is a risky enterprise, for it means that the universally accepted Jewish emphasis on the primacy of survival has to be questioned. The various movements in contemporary Jewry have to be subjected to critical

---

[5] ibid., p. 258.
[6] ibid., p. 259.

scrutiny. We must even dare to challenge the way we Jews regard the State of Israel and the Holocaust, and we must ask ourselves again what anti-Semitism really means to us. The aim is not to underestimate anything that is being done, but to show that Jewish activity without religious purpose is too limited and in the end may be self-defeating.

To survive is a *mitsvah*, a religious commandment, says Fackenheim. For him this means affirmation of the *Metsaveh*, the Commander, God. Those who today make Jewish survival the supreme commandment, do not appear to reflect a similar concern for God, the Supreme Commander. An Israeli educationalist of some distinction, Mordechai Bar-On, who for some time was responsible first for education in the Israeli Defence Forces, and then for youth education in the Diaspora under the auspices of the World Zionist Organization, has even set out to find an intellectual justification for a Judaism which insists on *mitsvot* but denies the *Metsaveh*.[7] It is a view akin to that of Reconstructionism in American–Jewish thought and yet another attempt to validate secularism in Judaism. Although Reconstructionism belongs, broadly speaking, to what has been labelled as Reform in this book, its naturalist theology makes it a particularly interesting exponent of secularism.

One of the arguments that is at times quoted in the debate about Jewish life without belief in God bases itself on the Rabbinic dictum, 'If they forsook even Me [i.e. God], all would turn out well, provided they kept studying my Torah.' The implication is that Jewish survival is safeguarded by observance and by Jewish education without reference to God. Modern Orthodoxy and Zionism often base their appeal to the masses on that assumption, and Reform – particularly in its Reconstructionist guise – has shown similar tendencies. In its classical manifestation it was not so much with observance and with education as with ethics that Reform Judaism tended to identify the Torah, but the implication was the same, namely that the question of God could be bypassed and yet a coherent picture of Judaism could be presented.

---

[7] See the Symposium in *Petahim*, quarterly Journal of Jewish Thought (in Hebrew with English summaries), Jerusalem, 3(36), September 1976.

It is, therefore, important that the Rabbinic dictum, referred to above, be quoted in full:

R. Huna and R. Jeremiah, citing R. Hiya ben Abba, said: It is written 'Your fathers . . . have forsaken Me and have not kept My Torah' (*Jeremiah* 16:11). If only they had kept *studying* My Torah! Indeed, if they forsook even Me, all would turn out well, provided they kept *studying* My Torah. *If they did forsake Me, yet kept on studying My Torah, its inner force, through their engagement with it, would be such as to bring them back to Me.*[8]

It is the *study* of Torah that is being stressed, not observance or even good deeds, and not as an aim in itself but as a means of returning to God. God is so concerned for His creatures that He is even prepared to put Himself in second place if that will bring His children back to Him: divine pathos calculated to combat human apathy.

Similarly, the liberal Reformers in their stress on ethical conduct tended to tamper with the message by not quoting Scripture in full. Their cardinal principle was the commandment (*Leviticus* 19:18), 'Love your neighbour as yourself.' But the full sentence continues: 'I am the Lord.' As we shall discuss later, Judaism knows no distinction between love of man and love of God, but it does insist that the former is meaningless without the latter. To cut short the verse in *Leviticus* and thus expurgate the reference to God is yet another manifestation of secularization. A radical critique of contemporary Judaism must include an exposure of such secularization and an insistence that God be restored to the consciousness of the Jew.

The assertion that it is not only possible, but legitimate, to be an observant Jew, perhaps belonging to an Orthodox synagogue, or to care for Jewish education, be it in the Diaspora or Israel, or to commit oneself to worthy causes, e.g. through one's membership of a non-Orthodox community, without reference to God must be challenged. It may be a necessary construction to retain the dogma of the supremacy of survival over all other concerns, but it may not be an authentic one

---

[8] *Pesikta De-Rab Kahana* 15:5, translated by W. G. Braude and I. J. Kapstein (JPSA, Philadelphia, 1975), p. 279. The italics are mine.

and, from the perspective of Prophetic radicalism, it is a dangerous one at that! A secular system of Jewish observance, however respectable and wholesome, a secular approach to Jewish education, however informative and enjoyable, a secular way of doing good deeds by Jews, however worthy and helpful, are alien to Judaism and distort its essence. Therefore, even the trauma of Auschwitz, the triumph of the Jewish State and the dual threat of anti-Semitism and assimilation must be viewed, as it were, from God's perspective, not only from the vantage point of the 'experts'. Sociology and psychology are no substitutes for theology, merely placebos for the secularists.

Consciousness of the span of Jewish history – not as a means to escape but as a source of inspiration to go forward – and awareness of our pain and the pain of others make us Jews God's witnesses in the world. The Prophetic stance of concern and compassion is the manifestation of that testimony. The secularist stress on survival by way of observance, education and ethics while ignoring the root of all three, namely God, has ominous implications for the future of Judaism. A radical critique in the vein of the Hebrew Prophets sets out to correct the secularist direction and to remind the Jew of the real nature of his testimony.

> My witnesses are you – declares the Lord –
> My servant whom I have chosen.
> To the end that you may take thought,
> And believe in Me,
> And understand that I am He:
> Before Me no god was formed,
> And after Me none shall exist –
> None but Me, the Lord.
> Beside Me, none can grant triumph.
> <div align="right">(<i>Isaiah</i> 43:10–11)</div>

13

A Battle on Three Fronts

A theology which takes divine pathos into account is a militant theology, reflected in the battles that the Biblical Prophets fought long ago. They fought on at least three fronts: against false prophets and the folly of premature messianism; against priests and the tyranny of ritualism; and against kings and the destructiveness of political power. Looking at the religious situation today, we find ourselves in the same three lines of battle: against those who ignore the need for moral renewal and naively believe that 'modernity' carries salvation; against those who insist that religion is identical with ritual and a code of behaviour; against those who make the spirit subservient to the needs of the State. Since this is a book about Judaism, it will confine itself to the struggle within it, but the basic division between the true Prophets and their opponents has universal application. Although my concern is to show that Prophetic Judaism must, inevitably, be critical of its modern exponents – classical Reform for its naive messianism; traditional Orthodoxy for its stress on ritual; political Zionism for its pre-occupation with power – others may wish to demonstrate the relevance of the Prophetic critique to other phenomena in contemporary society.

Johan Huizinga has, in another context, made a distinction between two kinds of players who go against the established rules of the game. The distinction well illustrates the difference between true and false prophets whose fundamental opposition to each other constitutes the first of the three lines of battle we are to consider. Huizinga calls them 'spoil sport' and 'cheat' respectively:

The player who trespasses against the rules or ignores them is a 'spoil-sport'. The spoil-sport is not the same as the false player, the cheat; for the latter pretends to be playing the game and, on the face of it, still acknowledges the magic circle. It is curious to note how much more lenient society is to the cheat than to the spoil-sport. This is because the spoil-sport shatters the play-world itself. By withdrawing from the game he reveals the relativity and fragility of the play-world in which he had temporarily shut himself with others. He robs play of its *illusion* – a pregnant word which means literally 'in-play' (from *inlusio*, *illudere*, or *inludere*). Therefore he must be cast out, for he threatens the existence of the play-community.[1]

The Biblical Prophet is the 'spoil-sport' *par excellence*. He 'shatters the play-world itself' and robs it of 'its illusion' by questioning the rules and the method. As a result, he is often removed from the community because he threatens its existence. The false prophet, by contrast, 'pretends to be playing the game' and gives the people what they want. To regard oneself as the heir of the true Prophets is to accept the responsibility to challenge the established rules of society, or the religious community, irrespective of the consequences. It is those who seek to emulate false prophets who give the masses what they want and promise them even more tomorrow. The current fashion in cults and fringe-religions is one of many modern manifestations of this kind of 'prophecy'.

The manifestations of false prophecy that should concern us in our context is that of classical Reform, which – consciously or otherwise – set out to give the assimilated Jew what he wanted. Despite its overt opposition to ritualism, Reform appeared to play the game according to the rules claiming to be the authentic custodian of pure Judaism. It was so pervasive and persuasive that it drowned the voice of true Prophecy. Its message of the dawn of a new, Messianic, era was so powerful, especially in the United States of America where the prospect of a millenium and a society foretold by Scripture was universally affirmed, that it was almost impossible to cast doubt on the veracity of the vision. What the Prophet heard when the people shouted, '*Shalom, shalom* – when there is no peace' (*Jeremiah* 6:14 and 8:11), many of us heard when Jewish assimilationists insisted that the era of

---

[1] Johan Huizinga, *Homo Ludens* (Paladin, London, 1970), p. 30.

universal brotherhood and peace was at hand. In their 'prophetic' hostility to ritualism they believed that, provided the peculiarities of Jewish life were minimized or eliminated, 'the ceremonial law' scrapped, Jews would become part of the Messianic epoch of enlightenment and tolerance.

The experience of the Holocaust – originating as it did in Germany, whose Jewry had been the principal exponent of this kind of 'prophecy' – has, of course, largely discredited the assimilationist doctrine. Its product, classical Reform, has changed. However, the strong antinomianism, which usually accompanies pseudo–Messianism, is still a strong component of Reform Judaism, particularly in the United States, which suggests that the battle against false prophets within the Jewish community itself is by no means over yet.

The description of true Prophets as 'spoil-sports' is not only apt in their relation to false prophets, the 'cheats', but even more so in their attitude to the priests, who had created 'the game' itself and were its custodians. Whereas the false prophets abused the rules to gain popularity and influence, the Prophets of the Bible challenged the system as such. They fought not only against the 'cheats' who promised a future that could never happen, but also against the professional priests who, through their obsession with the rules, made the present narrow and futile.

If classical Reform embodies elements of false prophecy, Orthodoxy has many traits that resemble those of the ancient priesthood. False prophets guarantee divine protection for no good reason; professional priests promise divine grace and social respectability as a reward for 'correct' behaviour. False prophets ignore the realities of the here and now by pointing to the future; professional priests are indifferent to the needs of the present by glorifying the past.

Such glorification is well illustrated both in Israel and in Britain, where Orthodoxy possesses more institutional power than its actual strength warrants. Despite the garb of modernity and the occasional Prophetic pronouncements on contemporary issues – notably those of the Orthodox Chief Rabbi in Britain – Orthodoxy is totally committed to the preservation of the past and the exercise of power through its insistence that 'the rules of the game' – proclaimed holy and immutable because they are 'hallowed by time' – be observed, irrespective

of circumstances. It is an approach that goes hand in hand
with the stress on survival, but it is inimical to a workable
definition of purpose. That is why Orthodox apologetics has
concentrated on preservation and not on renewal. That message appeals to the insecure and the confused who, in their
search for stability and certainty as an antidote to their own
confusion and their frightening perception of reality, cling to
every word of a formula that appears to be definite and immutable. It is, therefore, not surprising that 'mainstream' Orthodoxy, which demands relatively little from its supporters other
than a dogmatic disposition, attracts men and women who are
not fundamentalists but who, understandably, fear the new
and eschew battles with false prophets or dogmatic priests.
The Prophetic critique, in its efforts to formulate purpose, is
thus bound to stand in sharp opposition to the institutions of
contemporary Orthodoxy as well as to the predispositions of
many of its adherents.

It also stands in sharp opposition to the pursuit of political
power, which thus comes to constitute a third line of battle.
The Biblical Prophets fought every king who made morality
subservient to expediency. 'Prophecy was inherent in Israel;
monarchy was adopted,' writes David Polish[2] and, as a result,
the two invariably stand in a dialectical relationship. Those
who today regard themselves as exponents of Prophetic Judaism are bound to find themselves in a similar relationship
to political power, be it in the countries of the Diaspora where
they may live or in the Jewish State itself.

This does not mean that political power is to be despised,
for, as Polish puts it, 'the encounter of prophecy with power
was not for the purpose of displacing power but of taming it'.[3]
The religious perspective, to be true to itself, must act as a
corrective to the political thrust. As a result, the Jew committed to his tradition is likely to avoid the political arena,
not out of disloyalty to the State in which he lives but because
of his faithfulness to the religion he professes.

The same corrective and the same critique must also be
operative in relation to the Jewish State. However committed
we may be to Zionism as a doctrine, and to the State of Israel

[2] David Polish, 'Israel – The Meeting of Prophecy and Power', *The Year
Book of the Central Conference of American Rabbis*, lxxiv (1964), p. 161.
[3] ibid., p. 162.

as the epitome of Jewish renewal, we must not fail to recognize in both a tendency to use God for the sake of political gain, instead of using politics to achieve God's purpose. If Zionism, therefore, is to remain the catalyst of Jewish life today, it too must be open to a radical critique, not in order to be displaced but to be tamed.

It must now be our aim to identify some of the forces which in our century constitute something of the critique of the three movements in Judaism and, where appropriate, ally ourselves with them. Foremost among those forces is the life and work of Martin Buber. Buber, probably more than any other thinker in our century, has recognized the significance of the Prophetic critique and thus, obliquely or openly, engaged in battle on all three fronts. He was a modernist and yet had no time for Reform; he knew the Jewish past better than most and yet fought its unjustified imprisonment in Orthodoxy; he was an ardent Zionist and yet strongly opposed its quest for political power. In his lifetime, despite all his fame and prominence, he failed to influence Judaism significantly, and yet his analysis and his message remain our legacy. In the same way as the Biblical Prophets only became Israel's teachers long after their death, so the time will come when we will seek to understand Reform, Orthodoxy and Zionism from Buber's perspective. Generations will arise who will affirm with him that modernity is not flight into utopianism; that religion is not petrification into ritual; that the early pioneers did not drain the swamps in the Galilee and make the desert bloom in the Negev to end up subjugating the Arab inhabitants of Hebron on the grounds that the Biblical Patriarchs are buried there. Through Martin Buber, future generations will learn that modernity is not created by replacing the dogma of the immutability of the past with the one about the sanctity of the future; that authenticity consists not in fixed rules of behaviour but in open encounter with God; that sovereignty cannot be expressed in short-term political solutions but in long-term perspectives.

In the climate that currently prevails in the Jewish world it may be relatively easy to challenge the Reform perspective of the future, but it is difficult to question the Orthodox affirmation of the past, and almost impossible to be critical of the Zionist vision of the present. For the trauma of the Holocaust has made us sceptical of progress and imbued us with deep longing for what Hitler has destroyed, namely the world of East European Jewry. It has also created in us an almost total dependence, spiritual and physical, on the symbol of consolation, the State of Israel. If one wishes to be counted in Jewish life today, one may be critical of Reform, but one is expected to be deferential to Orthodoxy and totally accepting of all aspects of Israeli policy. It is a generally assumed axiom among contemporary Jews that, when you are fighting for survival, there is no time to voice intellectual reservations about Orthodox interpretations of the past or moral objections to this or that action by the government of Israel. Reform Judaism is almost invariably attacked, not on account of its teachings, but because it is seen as a threat to Jewish survival. And Reform defends itself, not by means of scholarship, seeking to demonstrate its case, but with statistics, showing that it preserves more and more Jews for Judaism.

For the sake of a more accurate perspective on what is happening in Jewish life today and what ought to be happening – in the Prophetic sense – tomorrow, we must dare to challenge the seemingly axiomatic assumptions that the tragedy of the Holocaust has imposed on us Jews. We must, to begin with, question the way in which the Holocaust itself is being interpreted in the Jewish world today, along the lines of Cordelia Edvardson's enquiry.

That it was the most monstrous crime committed against the Jewish people, perhaps against any people, should not be in dispute. The fact that the extent of the tragedy is already being denied by some, further confirms the suspicion that the destruction of six million Jews was not just a temporary aberration but a consistent effort to obliterate a people. Our response, therefore, must be a continuous re-statement of the crimes in all their sordid details. Every historian who brings further evidence of Nazi crimes to public knowledge not only hallows the memory of the martyrs, but also fights the messengers of inhumanity.

Our duty to teach the Holocaust, to remember the dead and to do all we can to prevent the tragedy happening again, is not in dispute. Nor is the effect of the trauma on all aspects of Jewish life to be devalued. But some Biblical Prophets, notably Jeremiah and Ezekiel, also witnessed Jewish tragedies, and for the eye-witness the relative size of a tragedy is immaterial. And yet, their experience of suffering, depletion and national humiliation did not persuade them to suspend self-criticism and moral judgment. On the contrary, the extreme situations in which they found themselves only heightened their sensitivity to truth and justice. True, they wanted to know and to understand what had happened and why, but, even more than that, they wished to put their grief and their trauma in the service of God, even when they challenged Him. If we take our role as heirs of the Prophets seriously, we must learn from them in our endeavours to fathom the Holocaust and thus not only seek to validate the Jewish struggle for survival but also to discern God's purpose. It is a very difficult task, but many of those who were there in the camps did not give up the quest for God. As Eliezer Berkovits has written:

> Many who were there lost their faith. I can understand them. A Hell fiercer than Dante's was their lot. I believe that God himself understands and does not hold their loss of faith against them. Such is my faith in God. Can I, therefore adopt their attitude for myself and rebel and reject? I was not there myself. I am not Job. I am only his brother. I cannot reject because there were others, too, in the thousands, in the tens of thousands, who were there and did not lose their faith; who accepted what happened to them in awesome submission to the will of God. I, who was not there, cannot reject, because to reject would be a desecration of the sacrifice of the myriads who accepted their lot in faith. How dare I reject, if they accepted![4]

To seek to comprehend something of the mystery of the presence of God in Auschwitz is to react Prophetically to the Holocaust. Chroniclers, poets and theologians have all attempted that and we can learn much from them, but not without Berkovits' *caveat*:

> In the presence of the holy faith of the crematoria, the ready faith of those who were not there, is vulgarity. But the disbelief of the sophisticated intellectual in the midst of an affluent society – in the light of the holy disbelief of the

---

[4] Eliezer Berkovits, *Faith after the Holocaust* (Ktav, New York, 1973), p. 4.

crematoria – is obscenity. We are not Job and we dare not speak and respond as if we were. We are only Job's brothers. We must believe, because our brother Job believed; and we must question, because our brother Job so often could not believe any longer.[5]

The tension between belief and questioning could easily lead to spiritual and physical inertia. But the Prophetic stance does not tolerate it. Instead it moves towards purposeful action, to an attempt at transformation of both the certainty and the doubt into the alleviation of human misery. In this respect the historians, the theologians and the poets fail us; we must turn to the psychotherapists, notably to Viktor Frankl and to Eugene Heimler.

Both Frankl and Heimler see in their personal experience in concentration camps the foundation of their respective methods of healing. It is because he had been in situations of extreme privation that Frankl is afterwards able to assert that 'suffering ceases to be suffering in some way at the moment it finds a meaning, such as the meaning of a sacrifice'. Out of this realization grows his unique method of therapy: 'It is one of the basic tenets of logotherapy that man's main concern is not to gain pleasure or to avoid pain but rather to see a meaning in his life. That is why man is even ready to suffer, on the condition, to be sure, that his suffering has a meaning.'[6] The experience of the Holocaust has here gone beyond history, theology and poetry to become a programme of action which sets out to find meaning, purpose and happiness even in suffering. Frankl's introduction to logotherapy, therefore, consists of two parts: the first is a moving record, full of profound psychological observations, of his concentration camp experience; the second is an account of his new method of healing which grew out of his earlier experience.

Eugene Heimler is even more explicit when he makes the connection between the war years and his subsequent work as a psychiatric social worker who is given the task to find a way of employing the unemployable in a London suburb: 'I thought of those who had survived the concentration camps

[5] ibid., p. 5.
[6] Viktor E. Frankl, *Man's Search for Meaning* (Hodder and Stoughton 1964), p. 115.

by finding some purpose for living, and I tried to see if it was possible to apply the same insights to the "work-shy" of Hendon.' [7] He did and went on to devise a method of turning tragedy into productive living, which he has termed 'social functioning'.

The work of Heimler, Frankl and others is relevant in our context, not only as an example of survivors who have been able to recover from their ordeal, but as a metaphor of how the Holocaust can be used: not merely as a way of labelling mental disorders (the survivor syndrome) and not only as a way of justifying the way Jewish life developed after the Second World War (the survival syndrome), but as a way of using the specific Jewish experience for a universal healing purpose. The interaction we often find in Prophetic literature between universalism and particularism has found here a tangible contemporary expression. The radical critique is thus not only confined to analysis, but it is constructive in the fullest sense of the word. The experience of pain brings with it the urge to alleviate pain; the highest aspirations of Judaism find here their practical expression.

The battles that the Biblical Prophets fought against false prophets, officious priests and unscrupulous kings were aspects of their total war against paganism. They identified in the antics of the ecstatic shamans, the sophisticated magicians and the hungry power-seekers, products of a world which does not know God and which, therefore, turns objects into gods. The Prophets were not intolerant towards their Gentile neighbours, but they recognized the insidious effect of paganism on the faith and the life of Israel and they knew that the tricks of false prophets, priests and kings alike were often manifestations of idolatry.

There is much to suggest that the paganism the ancients saw, both around them and within the institutions of their own religion and culture, is also in evidence today. We have referred to it here as secularism. Others have called it neo-paganism. Erich Fromm describes it as idolatry:

> An idol represents the object of man's central passion: the desire to return to the soil-mother, the craving for possession, power, fame, and so forth. The passion represented

---

[7] Eugene Heimler, *Mental Illness and Social Work* (Penguin 1967), p. 111.

by the idol is, at the same time, the supreme value within man's system of values . . . The history of mankind up to the present time is primarily the history of idol worship, from the primitive idols of clay and wood to the modern idols of the state, the leader, production and consumption – sanctified by the blessing of an idolized God.[8]

According to Fromm, idolatry – ancient and modern – is a form of self-worship:

Man transfers his own passions and qualities to the idol. The more he impoverishes himself, the greater and stronger becomes the idol. The idol is the alienated form of man's experience of himself. In worshipping the idol, man worships himself. But this self is a partial, limited aspect of man: his intelligence, his physical strength, power, fame, and so on. By identifying himself with a partial aspect of himself, man limits himself to this aspect; he loses his totality as a human being and ceases to grow. He is dependent on the idol, since only in submission to the idol does he find the shadow, although not the substance, of himself.[9]

The emphasis on survival over and above other considerations can also be seen as a collective manifestation of idolatry. The fact that it is the outcome of a tragedy and expressed out of the highest and most noble motives makes it especially difficult to criticize. Only the radical stance of the Prophets, the insiders, makes it possible for us to be critical and constructive at the same time.

By recognizing that much of what we find wanting in Reform Judaism, in neo-Orthodoxy and in Zionism is due to their overriding stress on survival and the result of inadvertent assimilation of contemporary paganism, we have attempted to give this radical critique a modern formulation. We are now ready for the task of reconstruction through the attempt to offer a profile of Judaism which looks beyond survival to seek its true purpose and is able to free itself from fairly artificial denominational divisions to find unity and real strength. If the first three branches of our Menorah are critical, the remaining four will be constructive. The fourth, and central,

[8] Erich Fromm, *You Shall Be As Gods* (Jonathan Cape 1967), p. 43.
[9] ibid., p. 43 f.

one will appropriately attempt to describe what commitment to God means to us today.

IV

GOD IN THE CENTRE

Man and his Maker in Perennial Dialogue

> Many of my fellow-countrymen do not
> believe in the existence of God. I am
> more modest. I do not believe in
> myself.
>
> Clive Sinclair[1]

---

[1] 'Ashkenazia' in *Encounter*, November 1980.

14

Three Fundamentals

Much has been written, particularly in the literature which can be described as Jewish apologetics, about the absence of any system of dogmas in Judaism. This is largely true, but nevertheless it cannot be denied that there are certain fundamental assumptions that are cardinal to Judaism. Thus the notion that God, Torah and Israel belong together is not just a slogan, or a homily, but a basic tenet of the Jewish faith. It is not really possible to speak of Judaism without reference to its monotheism, or its conviction that Torah is the means by which the One God communicates His will, or its understanding that it is the Jewish People that is the primary recipient of that will. However broadly these concepts may be interpreted, each has to be included in any presentation of Jewish belief. It would, for example, be inconceivable to describe Judaism as denying the existence of God, or eliminating the concept of Torah or refusing to take into account the unique role of Israel. Atheistic Judaism which has no view of Torah and does not ascribe any particular significance to the Jewish people is absurd.

There may be individuals who see themselves as non-believers, as totally uninterested and ignorant of the tradition, and as denying any specific characteristic to the Jewish people who, nevertheless, regard themselves as Jews, but they must be viewed as persons with idiosyncracies, not as exponents of Judaism. Such individuals, incidentally, often look for external secular criteria for their 'Judaism', reducing it to 'race'. In order to explain themselves they come to adopt Hitler's understanding of Jews, either in resignation or in defiance, leading to an odd mixture of self-hatred and a passion for 'Jewish defence'. Occasionally the defiant determination to describe oneself as a Jew without Judaism invokes the Holocaust, which thus becomes yet another screen to mask inner confusion. The late Isaac Deutscher was the most articulate exponent of that approach. In a conversation with the editor of a Jewish literary magazine,[1] he posed the rhetorical question whether Jewish consciousness was not 'a reflex, in the main, of anti-semitic pressures' and described Hitler as 'the greatest "re-definer" of the Jewish identity'. Although he refused to regard himself as a Jew on racial grounds, for that would have been a posthumous victory for Hitler, he could only define himself as a Jew because of Auschwitz:

> But if it is not race, what is it that makes a Jew? Religion? I am an atheist. Jewish nationalism? I am an internationalist. In neither sense am I, therefore, a Jew. I am, however, a Jew by force of my unconditional solidarity with the persecuted and exterminated.

This is a noble attempt to resolve a personal dilemma, but not sufficient for a definition. Even if Deutscher's Judaism was an enigma to himself, conditioned by his espousal of an ideology that denied it and a reality in which his environment foisted it upon him, we may be less confused on the matter: Isaac Deutscher was a Jew because he was born a Jew and, whether he liked it or not, he was a son of the Covenant that God made with His People and expressed in His Torah. Deutscher's extremely Orthodox Polish–Jewish parents imprinted it – literally – on his flesh through circumcision, which in Jewish tradition is described as *brith*, Covenant. In other words, even if the individual Jew may wish to explain his Judaism in the terms of reference of his ideology, or his historic situation, the mysterious interplay between God, Torah and Israel remains the true force that determines his identity. Deutscher's definition tells us a lot about himself, but not very much about Judaism.

Gershom Scholem, probably the greatest Jewish scholar in this century, recalling his life as a Zionist and student of mysticism, asserts: 'I have never cut myself off from God. I don't understand atheists; I never did. I think atheism is understandable only if you accept the rule of unbridled pas-

---

[1] 'The Jew in Modern Society – A Conversation with Isaac Deutscher', *The Jewish Quarterly*, xiii, 4(48) (Winter 1966), p. 7–12.

sions, a life without values.' [2] His understanding of the nature of Judaism is significant in our context:

> I cannot free myself from the dialectical lesson of history, according to which secularism is part of the process of our entry into history; entry into history means assimilating into it. Since I do not believe in 'like all the nations,' I do not see ultimate secularism as a possibility for us and it will not come to pass. I do not believe that we are going to liquidate ourselves. There is no reason for the Jews to exist like the Serbs. The Serbs have a reason to exist without theology, without an ahistorical dimension. If the Jews try to explain themselves only in a historical dimension, they will of necessity find themselves thinking about self-liquidation and total destruction.[3]

Isaac Deutscher in his attempt to defy Hitler by proclaiming his adherence to Judaism as an act of solidarity with the martyrs is, in fact, giving his enemy the posthumous victory he wishes to deny him. Only by recognizing another dimension to Jewish life – the mystical bond between God and His people – and not only the neurotic tangle between the Jews and their enemies, can Judaism be affirmed.

According to Scholem such an affirmation is not possible on rational grounds only. The great scholar of Judaism, for whom rational explanation and factual documentation is crucial in his work, nevertheless insists that 'reason is a great instrument of destruction. For construction, something beyond it is required.' [4] When pressed as to what that may be, he is somewhat vague, and yet he points to an essential truth:

> I don't know. Something that has – something moral. I don't believe there is an enduring rational morality; I don't believe it is possible to build a morality that will be an immanent network for Reason. I confess that in this respect I am what would be called a reactionary, for I believe that morality as a constructive force is impossible without religion, without some Power beyond Pure Reason. Secular

---

[2] Gershom Scholem, *On Jews and Judaism in Crisis* (Schocken, New York, 1976), p. 35.
[3] ibid., p. 34.
[4] ibid., p. 32.

morality is a morality built on Reason alone. I do not believe in this possibility. This is an utter illusion of philosophers, not to speak of sociologists.[5]

In Scholem's sense, this book too sets out to be reactionary – a reaction against the secularist and illusory clamour for survival. Instead, it attempts to recognize the interplay between the various elements in Judaism and to look at the future in terms of the relationship between them.

There are movements in Judaism which seek to minimize or deny one or more of the three basic elements, God, Torah and Israel. I have earlier suggested that Orthodoxy with its emphasis on Torah has tended to neglect God and, as a result, attracted many adherents who are *de facto* atheists but who justify their 'orthodoxy' because they see it as the most effective survival mechanism. The history of Reform suggests that its stress on God has tended to neglect the two other elements in the triad, and the fusion between secularism and Zionism has often resulted in a presentation of Judaism which leaves no room for God. It is on the basis of their failure to accept all three elements with equal emphasis that I have ventured to describe Orthodoxy, Reform and Zionism as inadequate to meet the real challenge of building the future of Judaism. My hope for the future of Judaism rests on the conviction that each of them can develop that which they have neglected and thus become authentic and complete. In so doing, incidentally, I also believe that the differences between them will greatly diminish. Sectarianism is in many ways the outcome of a partial affirmation of Judaism. To accept it in its totality is also to recognize the relative unimportance of the differences.

The three elements God, Torah and Israel, exist in a state of tension. God has significance only if His will is communicated (in Torah) to man who responds (Israel). Torah can only have meaning if it is the document that reflects the interaction between God and Israel. The Jewish People can only find its *raison d'être* as the community of faith that stands in a relationship of dialogue to God as manifest in Torah. The three concepts are thus not independent entities but a triad

---

[5] ibid.

that forms a unity. Those who fully uphold the triad also work for Jewish unity.

A state of tension, as Frankl has pointed out, is not a source of conflict but a sign of strength: 'What man actually needs is not a tensionless state but rather the striving and struggling for some goal worthy of him . . . If architects want to strengthen a decrepit arch, they *increase* the load which is laid upon it, for thereby the parts are joined more firmly together.'[6] Epicurus is said to have shunned religion because it did not offer peace of mind. If by that is meant a state in which tension is eliminated, he was undoubtedly correct. But, according to Frankl, existence without tension increases man's emotional instability. Neither does it make for theological coherence. Neat arguments are very often far removed from the truth.

In view of the fact that such a formulation can easily be misunderstood by Christians as an affirmation of the trinity, this is the place to assert that in no way are the two notions similar. At no time and under no circumstances is it suggested that Torah or Israel are of divine substance or co-equal with God. What is meant here is that any formulation of Judaism must include at least these three concepts and that none of them can be fully expressed in isolation from the others. We are, therefore, only concerned here with a method of discourse.

In the tension between God, Torah and Israel the true nature of Judaism can best be understood. None can claim the truth as its own; together they may approximate to it. Scholem's preoccupation with 'the dialectical lesson of history' is to be expanded into a view of Judaism as a whole, which sees the tenets of the faith, not as independent concepts to be defined rationally, but as inter-related ideas to be explored dialogically. Our critique of Jewish life today rests on the conviction that we have opted for slogans which can be put into neat compartments but which ultimately lead nowhere. The claim of any one movement to be the legitimate and sole heir of authentic Judaism has to be viewed with suspicion. Difficult though it may seem, both Jewish existence and Jew-

[6] Viktor E. Frankl, *Man's Search for Meaning* (Hodder and Stoughton 1964), p. 107.

ish belief have to be viewed dialectically as a struggle between seemingly opposing forces. The truth must be sought in the paradox, not in the neat rational formulation. A Judaism of the future, seeking to define its purpose rather than merely devising strategies for self-preservation, will be expressed in this way. And in the tension we may discover its fundamental unity.

15

Jacob and the Angel: The Jew Before God

The interpretation of the encounter between Jacob and Esau, offered in Chapter 1, is one of many that tradition provides. Characteristically, Judaism does not 'authorize' one and discard any other, because it does not wish to reduce its teachings to slogans. Instead, it offers us an intricate picture of many options and inter-relations. In addition, each interpretation is in itself an expression of a dialectical relationship. Thus the one in which the mysterious being is identified as 'the guardian angel of Esau' illustrates the relationship between the Jew and the non-Jewish world. It is Scholem's 'dialectical lesson of history'. In this chapter, wherein we attempt to explore the relationship between God and Israel through the words of the Torah, we turn to the more literal interpretation of the Biblical story.

The account in Scripture concludes with the mysterious being that wrestles with Jacob assuring the Patriarch that 'your name shall no longer be Jacob, but Israel, for you have striven with beings divine and human, and have prevailed' (*Genesis* 32:29). The text then tells us that 'Jacob names the place Peniel, meaning "I have seen a divine being face to face, yet my life has been preserved" ' (*Genesis* 32:31). Bearing in mind the various interpretations, Elie Wiesel urges his readers to opt for the literal one:

> And yet it would be equally acceptable to give a more literal interpretation to the text and suggest that at Peniel, Jacob was forced into battle not with a human being or an angel, or even a self-image, but with Him who encompasses us all. Though almost unanimously rejected by Talmudic tradition, this hypothesis deserves close scrutiny. After all, Ja-

cob himself lent it veracity: he himself never spoke of man or angel, or self-reflection. He spoke of God.[1]

Wiesel concludes, therefore, that 'like his father and grand-father, he wanted to engage God in dialogue, no matter how great the risk. It was God he wished to confront.'[2]

Elie Wiesel, the chronicler of the concentration camps and the spokesman of the survivors, sees the Patriarch as 'the son of a survivor'[3] who 'needed to provoke God to justify his place in history. Only thus could he surpass himself and become Israel.'[4] The blind obedience of Isaac, his father, at Moriah had to give way to a dialogue with God in search of his own identity. That is Wiesel's paradigm for Jewish exist-ence after the Holocaust. The old categories no longer make sense. Survival as such is not sufficient. The children of sur-vivors have to take risks in order to receive God's blessing and find their own identity as Israel. In Wiesel's words: 'From his contest with God, Jacob emerged triumphant but limping; he was never to be the same again.'[5]

Some survivors and children of survivors have tended to misunderstand the contest as a battle and regard it as their duty to accuse and to abuse God. They have falsely taken upon themselves the mantle of Job whereas, as Berkovits reminds us, we can only claim to be Job's brother. The dialectic is not a contest but a dialogue. As suggested earlier in this chapter, Jewish existence cannot write God out of the script of Judaism. But, at the same time, children of survivors cannot slavishly accept and affirm the God of their grandpar-ents and parents. They have to encounter Him anew, as Jacob did.

Jewish tradition has always believed that each generation has to experience God in its own way. The Amidah, the prayer devout Jews recite three times a day, praises God as 'the God of Abraham, the God of Isaac and the God of Jacob' and not 'the God of Abraham, Isaac and Jacob', because each of the Patriarchs had to come to terms with 'his' God. To merely

---

[1] Elie Wiesel, *Messengers of God* (Pocket Books, New York, 1977), p. 139.
[2] ibid., p. 141 f.
[3] ibid., p. 142.
[4] ibid., p. 143.
[5] ibid., p. 139.

'take over' God as encountered by earlier generations is not enough. That is why the same prayer speaks of 'Lord our God, *and* God of our fathers'. We have to go through the same process that our fathers did in order to establish our identity as Israel. That does not mean that God changes, but that man's approach to Him is different in every age. As a result, the relationship is different and our perception of Him is unique to each one of us: 'With the loyal You deal loyally: with the blameless hero, blamelessly. With the pure You act in purity, and with the perverse You are wily. To humble folk You give victory, and You look with scorn on the haughty.' (2 *Samuel* 22:26–8).

Martin Buber's thought is based on the notion that reality is what happens *between* partners in dialogue, both on the human plane and in the encounter between God and man. It therefore offers a framework for our religious self-understanding which expresses ancient wisdom in a contemporary idiom. Only when I can enter into a relationship with the Eternal Thou, which is a metaphor for God, does the reality known as 'religion' (although Buber himself does not like that word) unfold itself. In the encounter at Peniel God affirmed Jacob, blessed him and gave him a new name. In response, the Patriarch affirmed his Maker, made Him 'his' God. To emulate this pattern is to fathom Ultimate Reality.

Buber would insist that dialogue is the very opposite of mysticism, but his poetic language is enigmatic and thus difficult to grasp and even more difficult to put into practice. His notion of *I–thou*, the relationship between man and man, and its basis for the dialogue with the Eternal Thou, the relationship between God and man, is difficult. It becomes a little easier to grasp when we explore its alternative: the *I–it* relationship. Whereas *I–thou* reflects a dialogue between subjects who both have a will and both mutually affirm each other, *I–it* is the model for the relationship between subject and object, a metaphor for manipulation, particularly apt in the age of technology. We know what we do with objects. That should enable us to fathom the extent of the disaster we cause when we relate to persons as if they were objects. This should also help us to envisage what happens when we treat God as an *it*, as a concept or a thing – in fact, an idol – and do not address Him as the Eternal Thou.

This means that Buber's scheme for dialogue is not to be viewed as idyllic and harmonious, but as a struggle and a fight. One of the many misconceptions about religion is the belief that being religious is to be free from problems and difficulties. The testimony of the Biblical Prophets, however, should dispel any such notion. True encounter is a struggle 'for the sake of Heaven'.

Prophetic Judaism with its abhorrence of idolatry teaches us dialogue; contemporary society and thought with its stress on 'objectivity' makes for manipulation. Our search for a dialectical formulation of Judaism to be expressed in terms of Prophetic radicalism leads us to Buber's basic model and to an affirmation of the formula that God cannot be *expressed*, only *addressed*. When we seek to define God, we limit Him; the very attempt to express Him leads us to idolatry. Only in the encounter between the human person and the personal God is religious reality possible. A Judaism that seeks to go beyond the quest for mere survival must begin with a new appreciation of that encounter. By creating the kind of communities in which human dialogue is possible, something of the real dialogue between God and man may be perceived. By founding communities for intrinsic reasons rather than as tools for Jewish survival, such dialogue is at least potentially possible.

Our understanding that God cannot be *expressed*, but must be *addressed*, suggests, according to D.W.D. Shaw,[6] that the religious search is a response to the question, '*Who* is God?', not '*What* is God?'. The 'idolatry' of philosophers and theologians consists in seeking to objectify God and then define Him in answer to 'objective' questions. Those who wish to enter into dialogue with Him relate to Him personally and, therefore, seek to answer the personal question. The *impasse* of contemporary religious thought, it is further implied, has come about because right answers have been given to wrong questions; what is now required is a direct response (which is more than an answer) in the immediate encounter. Martin Buber has become our mentor in our efforts to recognize such encounters. By helping us to find them in our relationships to people, he points the way to finding them in our relation-

[6] D. W. D. Shaw, *Who is God?* (SCM 1968).

JACOB AND THE ANGEL: THE JEW BEFORE GOD   101

ship to God: it is not surprising that understanding of Scripture is, therefore, so central to his teaching.

The connection between the social and the religious has to be stressed. Religious experience, the opportunity to address God and to be addressed by Him, is available to all through the opportunities for human encounter in society. That is why the community is not just to be the institution that fosters survival, but also the place where man's true purpose can be discerned. And just as in the community, encounter means not only consent but also struggle, so in the relationship to God, wrestling is as indigenous as is obedience, and perhaps much more honest.

He whose sole aim is survival will undoubtedly concentrate on the scientific efforts to answer the question, '*What* is God?', or more likely, 'What *was* God?' Historicism has played an important part in contemporary Jewish theology. With the help of meticulous scholarship, tomes have been written cataloguing the beliefs of the ancestors and, by implication, showing why they are not relevant now. In these books God is almost invariably reduced to an object, an *it*. Those who now look at purpose beyond survival must find their way back to the personal encounter, to the question, '*Who* is God?', putting equal and maximum stress on each of the three words. The result of this enquiry will not lead to a theory, but to a response, which will come about through struggle. Theories can be adjusted and formulated to appear neat and consistent; actual encounters are much less tidy and much more likely to lead to the kind of situation in which Jacob found himself at Peniel.

The struggle is likely to be particularly fierce when survivors from the concentration camps and their children and grandchildren engage in it. Then the question is no longer going to be, '*Who* is God?' or '*What* is God?' but '*Where* is God?', and 'Where was He at Auschwitz?' In the face of such questions, even Buber has to modify his perception of dialogue and, using Biblical language, speak of God who 'hides His face'. But if He hid His face then, what does He want with us now? The experience of the Holocaust has made many give up the struggle for purpose; they are not able to struggle with God. It is to them and for them that Wiesel speaks when he stresses the notion of the inescapable battle with God rather than an idyllic encounter, as perhaps Buber would have wanted it. According to Wiesel, 'the Jew may rise against God, provided he remains with God'.[7] The Biblical Job may have risen against God – he definitely rose against those who spoke in ready-made formulae in the name of God, i.e. the theologians, the idolators of his day and perhaps also ours – but he always remained with God. As Job's brothers, in Berkovits' terminology, we have no right to do less.

However, the problem of theodicy cannot be dismissed with poetry, even if it reflects testimonies as powerful as the writings of Martin Buber, Elie Wiesel, Eliezer Berkovits and many others. Theology, with its attempt to objectify and explain, reduces us to the status of one of Job's friends. As his brothers more is expected of us. In the best tradition of the Kabbalists, we have to accept the reality of evil and struggle with it. When the Messiah comes, the mystery of evil will be resolved, but what are we to do in the meantime? Explain it away? Turn our face away from God? Submit?

Perhaps a little of each of these possibilities has to be explored in characteristic dialectic fashion: explain *and* argue; submit *and* rebel. But, above all, try to eradicate evil, or at least to diminish it. Purpose inevitably leads to action. Despite the agony of suffering and doubt, through the *I–thou* relationship in society and the glimpse of a relationship to the Eternal Thou, man is moved to act to diminish the suffering, even if he cannot eradicate the doubt.

The performance of *mitsvot*, not only ceremonial but, above all, moral commandments, offers every Jew an opportunity to diminish evil. In the same way that it is impossible to have the *mitsvah* without the *Metsaveh*, the *commandment* without the *Commander*, so it is impossible to address God without responding through action. In this respect we move beyond Buber and Wiesel to A. J. Heschel, who was not only a theologian but a rabbi, a teacher of rabbis, an observant Jew. For Heschel 'the Biblical answer to evil is not the good but the *holy*'. He sees it as 'an attempt to raise man to a higher level of a existence, where man is not alone when confronted

---

[7] 'Jewish Values in the Post-Holocaust Future' – a symposium in *Judaism*, xvi, 3 (Summer 1967), p. 299.

with evil'.[8] And even more explicitly: 'The *mitsvah*, the humble single act of serving God, of helping man, of cleansing the self, is our way of dealing with the problem. We do not know how to solve the problem of *evil*, but we are not exempt from dealing with evils.' [9]

To encounter God, to struggle with Him, does not lead to theoretical solutions, but to practical actions in which our purpose as human beings is revealed and, through the concept of *mitsvah*, our role as Jews defined. By carrying out commandments there is no need to introduce a new hierarchy in which the commandment not to give Hitler a posthumous victory takes precedence; every commandment carried out serves that purpose. This does not mean that reason has to be abdicated, but it can, and must, be transcended, if Judaism is to face its future with confidence:

> We are not called upon to abdicate reason and reflection in pondering on the nature of evil and comprehending as much of it as we can. What still remains a mystery may then be borne with resignation in a world where so much may be experienced with joy. Man's efforts must never cease to transform the evil in the world and reduce its dimensions. Yet what cannot be transformed can be transcended, through the vision of a world which is the handiwork of God.[10]

The future of Judaism after the Holocaust depends on the ability of individuals, survivors and the children and grandchildren of survivors, to imitate Jacob at Peniel and wrestle with God. It is not a coincidence that it is Elie Wiesel, the spokesman of survivors, who has come to stress this interpretation of the text. Once we have engaged in that struggle we may perceive the presence of God, contrary to our fear that at Auschwitz He finally abandoned us. By engaging in dialogue, as understood by Martin Buber, we may be able to share the philosopher's vision, couched in Biblical language, that God did not abandon us, but in His infinite mystery hid His face for a brief moment.

[8] A. J. Heschel, *God in Search of Man* (Meridian, New York, 1959), p. 376.
[9] ibid., p. 377.
[10] Robert Gordis, *A Faith for Moderns* (Bloch, New York, 1960), p. 189.

In Buber's scheme of things, the encounter with God is only possible through encounters with fellow men. The community is, therefore, a crucial factor in the revival of Judaism, not merely as a way of keeping together its members and preserving the past, but as the *milieu* in which the future can be shaped. The community, then, is the environment which makes it possible for the individual *I* to address the Eternal *Thou* and to be addressed by Him. The outcome of that encounter leads to the *mitsvah*, the commandment, in the widest sense of the word. The stress is on the ethical, for it is this which shows us a way of transcending evil by helping to eradicate it rather than withdrawing because of its magnitude.

We will have reason to return both to the significance of community and the centrality of *mitsvah* in later chapters. But we note now that the radical response to the crisis in Jewish life today does not consist of introducing radically new ideas. It is, rather, a restatement of what has always been in the centre of Judaism: dialogue, community, commandment. That is the radicalism of the Prophets: to unmask what Buber would have called the *I–it* and to replace it with the *I–thou*. It is the objectification, of which all the streams within contemporary Judaism are guilty, that has led us astray, not the basic teachings of our tradition. By seeking to restate these teachings and to re-discover their dynamics we are attempting to plan for the future. By stressing the dimension of dialogue, not dogma, of struggle, not certainty, we are reflecting the needs of modern man and pointing to the possibility of belief beyond scepticism and apathy.

16

God Before Us

D. W. D. Shaw has written that 'perhaps, today, we can best envisage God as ahead of us, awaiting us in the open future that lies before us, beckoning us on, as it were, with our fellow men, not out of fear, or magic, or determined power, but out of love'.[1] Much of what has been written in this chapter has been an attempt to indicate how this is possible after Auschwitz, and why such a vision is essential, if we are to face the future with confidence. Let us now attempt to point to areas in religious thought which require a change in terminology, if we are to recognize God when we encounter Him.

Jewish tradition knows of no adequate definition of God, since a definition is (as the word suggests) a limitation and thus an objectification (an *it*, in Buber's terminology) and a demotion of God (idolatry, as Fromm would have it). Therefore, when Moses asks for God's name when he is addressed by Him at the Burning Bush, he is told; '*Ehyeh-Asher-Ehyeh*, I am the Ever-Present' and urged to say to the Israelites, '*Ehye* sent me to you' (*Exodus* 3:14). Similarly, when he later pleads with God, 'Oh, let me behold Your Presence!' (*Exodus* 33:18), he is told, 'You cannot see My face, for man may not see Me and live' (*Exodus* 33:20).

Definition is, therefore, not possible, but God is known through history. Thus when refusing to disclose His name, i.e. His essence, God nevertheless says to Moses: 'Thus shall you speak to the Israelites: The Lord, the God of your fathers, the God of Abraham, the God of Isaac, and the God of Jacob, has sent me to you: this shall be My name forever, this My appellation for all eternity' (*Exodus* 3:15). It is this appella-

---

[1] Shaw, op. cit., p. 80.

tion, 'the God of Abraham, the God of Isaac, and the God of Jacob' which has found its way to the liturgy and given rise to the explanation which stresses the dynamic nature of God, as discussed earlier in this chapter. Even the Ten Commandments offer no definition of God beyond the historic evidence, which is the sole reason for His uniqueness: 'I the Lord am your God who brought you out of the land of Egypt, the house of bondage: You shall have no other gods beside Me' (*Exodus* 20:2–3).

Jewish thought reflects a constant tension between, on the one hand, the need to describe God as concretely as possible, for He is the living God, and, on the other, the fear that every such description limits Him and turns Him into an idol. We have not resolved the tension and never will. We can, however, limit some of the pitfalls of 'God-talk' by being conscious of the dichotomy and by re-examining the terminology. To do what many of those who have put Jewish survival before anything else have done, namely to insist that Judaism has no time for theology, is to escape the problem rather than to tackle it. It has been a welcome escape for those who have sought to secularize Judaism in the name of the Jewish 'religion'. I have suggested before that it is difficult to see how a Jew can find purpose in his existence without encountering God. Let me now add the obvious: that it is difficult to see how that encounter can be described and shared without the use of language. The *mitsvah* may indeed transcend the problem of evil, and silence may be a way of communicating with God, but no religious education is possible without articulating that experience to others. Even mystics have written tracts, or made their disciples do it, and the Hebrew for Prophet, *navi*, means 'speaker'. So speak we must, even though we recognize that each word we use about God says nothing about His essence, which is beyond our grasp, but tells us something about His attributes, which are within our reach. Although it may not be possible to describe who God *is* – for that becomes only revealed in the actual encounter – it is possible to state what He *does* and thus offer a formula for action to those in search: 'You shall be holy, for I, the Lord your God, am holy' (*Leviticus* 19:2).

Many of the terms are sufficiently broad to offer themselves to reinterpretation without major theological revisions. The word 'king' does not mean to a child today what it meant to his ancestors, but he knows enough about history to read 'ruler' for 'king' and be contented without having to change the ancient terminology. Similarly, all attempts to replace 'The Lord is my shepherd' (*Psalms* 23:1) with 'The Lord is my astronaut' have been met with the ridicule they deserve. However, there is one area of 'God-talk' which needs drastic revision if all Jews are to have the *a priori* opportunity to encounter God. It is not a mere question of grammar or vocabulary, but much else is involved. I refer to the purely masculine perception of God in traditional religion and the difficulties which that has created in the light of the feminist revolution of today. In our attempt to consider a future of Judaism which centres on God as much as on People, we cannot escape this issue. It is even legitimate to surmise that one factor in the secularist flight from God has been the inability to relate the concept of the equality of the sexes to traditional theology.

Judaism has always been a masculine religion. It has spoken of God as He, never as She. Idols are often described as goddesses, but the God of the fathers is 'male'. In the dialectical scheme of things, Israel, the partner of God, should have been feminine thus giving credence to the Prophetic image of marriage, so often used to describe the relationship between God and His People. If God is the bridegroom, Israel should be the bride, as the Rabbinic interpretation of the Song of Songs implies. The observant Jew, as he winds the straps of one of the phylacteries round his finger at morning prayers repeats God's assurance to His People: 'And I will espouse you forever: I will espouse you with righteousness and justice, and with goodness and mercy, and I will espouse you with faithfulness; then you shall be devoted to the Lord' (*Hosea* 2:21–2).

However, it is only a man who would put on the phylacteries. Traditional Judaism may not explicitly bar a woman from doing so, but she is under no obligation and this means, at least in the circles where such rituals are observed, that she is prohibited. The imagery of the marriage in which God is the bridegroom and Israel the bride is reflected in a ritual in which those representing the bride are exclusively male. Israel, God's bride, is named after Jacob the Patriarch! There is thus an inherent inconsistency in the dialogical relationship which has tended to exclude women, which now has to be recognized in the light of the radically changed role of women in the world.

Although both God and Israel are conceived as masculine in traditional Judaism, and despite the fact that the Prophets describe the relationship as a marriage, and the language used has strong sexual overtones – for the Christian distinction between *eros* and *agape*, love of man and love of God, is almost unknown in Judaism – there is no indication whatsoever that a 'homosexual' relationship between God and Israel is envisaged. Such a relationship would be regarded as illicit. The contradiction which thus arose has resulted in much confusion in the religious life of Jews. It has forced us to seek God-substitutes in order to escape the image of a cosmic 'marriage' between two male partners, God and Israel.

Jewish tradition has tried to resolve the problem by distinguishing between conceptual and symbolic thinking. One manifestation of the latter is *Shechinah*, the Divine Presence, described as referring to 'the numinous immanence of God in the world' and as 'God viewed in spatiotemporal terms as a presence, particularly in a this worldly context'.[2] The literature repeatedly points out that it is not a question here of challenging the monotheistic notion of God, but merely of finding a more adequate manifestation of His Presence. The fact that this manifestation is feminine is not a coincidence. If God is to be perceived as a force in this world relating to Israel, a feminine word makes such a perception easier. The mystics recognized this and it was in Kabbalistic literature that the *Shechinah* came to play an important part. That is how Scholem describes the shift from the Rabbinic to the Kabbalistic understanding:

> In Talmudic literature and non-Kabbalistic Rabbinical Judaism, the *Shekhinah* – literally in-dwelling, namely of God in the world – is taken to mean simply God himself in His omni-presence and activity in the world and especially in Israel. God's presence, what in the Bible is called His 'face', is in Rabbinical usage His *Shekhinah*. Nowhere in the older literature is a distinction made between God himself and

[2] *Encyclopaedia Judaica*, Jerusalem 1971, vol. 14:134g.

His *Shekhinah*; the *Shekhinah* is not a special hypostasis distinguished from God as a whole. It is very different in the usage of the Kabbalah . . . Here the *Shekhinah* becomes an aspect of God, a quasi-independent feminine element within Him.[3]

Scholem fully recognizes the significance of the Kabbalistic dimension:

The discovery of a feminine element in God, which the Kabbalists tried to justify by gnostic exegesis, is of course one of the most significant steps they took. Often regarded with the utmost misgiving by strictly Rabbinical, non-Kabbalistic Jews, often distorted into inoffensiveness by embarrassed Kabbalistic apologists, this mystical conception of the feminine principle of the *Shekhinah* as a providential guide of Creation achieved enormous popularity among the masses of the Jewish people, so showing that here the Kabbalists had uncovered one of the primordial religious impulses still latent in Judaism.[4]

These impulses made the symbolic description of the relationship between God and Israel meaningful and real and, despite the embarrassment, legitimate and proper. The Kabbalistic idea now found its ritual expression in the recitation of the concluding section of the Book of Proverbs, 'which seems to sing the praises of the noble housewife and her activities, but which the Kabbalists interpreted line by line as a hymn to the *Shekhinah*'.[5]

That it is not so much a question of discovering the feminine element in God as it is to establish a partner of the opposite sex in this all-pervasive cosmic relationship, is borne out by the fact that sometimes the description of the community of Israel is transferred to the *Shechinah*. It is as if even the Kabbalists could not bear to see themselves as feminine and thus projected the description of the people on to God:

Nowhere does the Talmudic literature identify the *Shekhinah* with the Ecclesia. In the Kabbalah, however, it is

---

[3] Gershom G. Scholem, *On the Kabbalah And Its Symbolism* (Routledge and Kegan Paul 1965), p. 104f.
[4] ibid., p. 105.
[5] ibid., p. 142.

precisely this identification that introduces the symbolism of the feminine into the sphere of the divine. Through this identification, everything that is said in the Talmudic interpretations of the Song of Songs about the Community of Israel as daughter and bride was transferred to the *Shekhinah*.[6]

In the same way as the Kabbalists were able to discover the feminine element in God, we now may be able to recognize the feminine element in ourselves. That is not only of importance to the Jewish attitude to women and to homosexuality, but central to Judaism's perception of the relationship between God and man. In the light of the feminist revolution, such a step should be possible. By accepting the feminine in Israel, we may be able to recognize the masculine in God and appreciate the depth of the relationship between the two. Feminists are missing the point when they insist that God should not be exclusively masculine; the Kabbalists did that long before them – for decidedly anti-feminist reasons: to retain their masculinity intact. The real opportunity of the feminist revolution is to recognize the feminine side of Israel and thus help *her* (Israel) to relate to *Him* (God). It is, therefore, theologically much more important to accept women as rabbis than it is to describe God as *she*. In the former situation, the place of women *qua* women in Israel has been accepted; in the latter, the women merely imitate the men and perpetuate the imbalance and the injustice.

Emmanuel Lévinas, in his essay on the feminine element in Judaism,[7] suggests that the Kabbalistic notions of the *Shechinah* 'are not taken seriously'. Instead, he insists that it is in *human* affairs that the feminine has its place:

The Biblical events would not have gone forward as they did but for their watchful clarity, the toughness of their determination, and their cunning and spirit of sacrifice. The world in which these events transpired would not have been structured as it was – and as it still is and always will be – but for the secret presence, to the verge of invisibility, of these mothers, these wives and daughters, but for their

---

[6] ibid., p. 106.
[7] Emmanuel Lévinas, 'Judaism and the Feminine Element', in *Judaism*, xviii, 1 (Winter 1969), pp. 30–8.

silent footsteps in the depth and opaqueness of reality, depicting the dimensions of interiority itself and making the world habitable.

However, whereas in the past women could only exist on 'the verge of invisibility', we are now facing a future 'far from the conditions of the Orient where, at the heart of a masculine civilization, woman finds herself entirely subordinate to the masculine will or reduced to charming or gladdening the austere life of men'. Therefore, the feminine element can be openly acknowledged and affirmed thus allowing the relationship between God and His people to reach its full potential.

The Kabbalists spoke of the *Shechinah*, the feminine element of God, being in exile and our duty to restore it to its masculine counterpart to make Redemption possible. Viewing the history of Judaism in the light of the present changes in our appreciation of women, we can speak of the feminine dimension of Israel being in exile and our duty to restore it to its masculine counterpart for the sake of proper encounter between the God of Abraham, the God of Isaac and the God of Jacob and their descendants, so that the God of our Fathers is also recognized as the God of our Mothers and thus *our* God in the fullest sense of the word.

This in itself may not secure the future of Judaism, but it will restore the central of its three components, God, to the living and loving partner that He is, without having to create the *Shechinah* to be able to speak of His immanence, but by addressing Him as the Eternal Thou. The effort to integrate women in the Reform interpretation of Judaism into our religious consciousness is, therefore, of historic significance and an important indication that it may be able to free itself from the secularization that threatens it.

Our understanding of God is bound up with our understanding of Torah and Israel. Our relationship to Him is one of dialogue, and the Torah is a record of it through our history as well as a pointer to how it is to be conducted in the future. Only by understanding ourselves as Israel are we able to speak of God and relate to Him. These are the three central theses of this chapter. The third point has been formulated, more generally, by Fackenheim:

The method of modern Jewish theology must differ from

that of classical theology. This latter 'worked its way down,' i.e., assumed from the start what to modern man is the thing most in question: the actuality of a divine revelation given to man and Israel. Modern theology must 'work its way up,' i.e., show, by an analysis of the human condition, that man's existence, properly understood, forces him to raise the question of the Supernatural, and the existential problem of the 'leap into faith'.

Fackenheim concludes, therefore, that 'the analysis of the human condition constitutes the necessary prolegomenon for all modern Jewish and, indeed, all modern theology'.[8]

Berger distinguishes between the traditional and the modern approach to God, that of the past and that of the future, by differentiating between 'inductive faith' and 'deductive faith'. He defines the former as 'a religious process of thought that begins with facts of human experience' and states that the latter 'begins with certain assumptions (notably assumptions about divine revelation) that cannot be tested by experience'.[9] It is Berger's contention that human experience offers a wealth of 'signals of transcendence', i.e. 'phenomena that are to be found within the domain of our "natural" reality but that appear to point beyond that reality'.[10] By picking up such signals we are able to communicate with God, address Him without knowing His essence. The future of Judaism depends, therefore, on our ability to receive and to transmit. Like Noah, we can only hope to survive the deluge by 'walking with God'. (*Genesis* 6:9). As the Prophet proclaimed:

> He has told you, O man, what is good
> And what the Lord requires of you.
> Only to do justice
> And to love goodness
> And to walk humbly with your God
> Then will your name achieve wisdom.
>   (*Micah* 6:8–9)

Our aim is neither philosophic proof nor blind faith, be-

---

[8] Emil L. Fackenheim, *Quest for Past and Future* (Indiana University Press, Bloomington & London, 1968), p. 101.

[9] Peter L. Berger, *A Rumour of Angels*, (Penguin 1971), p. 75f.

[10] ibid., p. 70.

cause they are not really attainable. Instead, we seek to face the future by learning to trust, and we base this trust on the understanding of our condition as human beings and as Jews. We are not called upon to act but to be. In the words of Ignaz Maybaum:

> Trust is unconditional trust. Trust has no aim, whereas every action has its aim. To walk humbly before God, includes many things which must be done, and many things which must not be done. By itself, this humbly walking before God is not an action. It is an attitude.[11]

It is this attitude that made it possible for Abraham to face Satan in the distant past, and it is the same attitude that will enable us to affirm God today and tomorrow.

[11] Ignaz Maybaum, *The Sacrifice of Isaac* (Vallentine, Mitchell 1959), p. 9f.

V

IN THE LIGHT OF THE TORAH
Jewish Teaching as Universal Wisdom

> I make this covenant, with its sanctions,
> not with you alone, but both with those
> who are standing here with us this day
> before the Lord our God and with those
> who are not with us here this day.
>
> *Deuteronomy* 29:13–14

17

Torah as Love-Letter and Marriage Contract

The masculine self-understanding of Patriarchal Judaism has forced it to find a feminine image of God in order to express symbolically the relationship between Him and His people. A radical restatement demands, therefore, a revision of the Patriarchal self-understanding by recognizing the feminine element in Israel. The current efforts of Reform to do so carry the promise of a religious revival; one can already point to the impact of the participation of women as equals in both worship and management in Reform congregations. That has happened even before women rabbis have had an opportunity to influence the character of non-Orthodox Judaism. There is still a danger, of course, that instead of stressing the feminine element, women will merely seek to imitate men. However, despite some signs to that effect, it is reasonable to assume that this is only temporary, and that very soon women will behave as women, not as subservient marginal figures in the life of the Jewish people, but as equals in every sense of the word.

Jewish Patriarchal attitudes led not only to a distortion of the divine through the introduction of the *Shechinah*, but they also resulted in a concept of Torah which deserves our consideration. Traditional, masculine, Judaism views the Torah in feminine terms. It discourages women handling the Scroll containing the Five Books of Moses whereas men are encouraged to cuddle and kiss it. On the festival of *Simchat Torah* (Rejoicing of the Torah) the men called up to the reading of the last portion in the old cycle and the first reading of the new one are described as *chatanim*, bridegrooms. The celebration that follows often reminds one of a wedding feast. By viewing the Torah as female, the rabbis could express something that they were unable to manifest in their relationship to God. Although it would be totally wrong to accuse them of consciously seeking to replace God with the Torah, it is difficult not to recognize unconscious expressions to this effect. Rabbinic Judaism in a way shifted the emphasis from the relationship between Israel and God to the relationship between Israel and the *Word* of God.

Traditional Judaism seems to relate to that Word with the immediacy of an *I–thou* relationship, analogous to the ideal relationship with God. That may have been due to the inability of a masculine society to relate to the masculine God in a way that it could do to a feminine Torah. Thus what the *Shechinah* was to the mystics, the Torah became to the rationalists. To study and, therefore, to relate to the Torah is the highest ideal that Jewish tradition puts before each of its sons, but it actively discourages such involvement in its daughters. Study is seen as an activity designated for men, not for women. There is something unseemly, in the eyes of tradition, in women studying Torah; perhaps some of the opposition to women rabbis, even on the part of non-Orthodox Jews, stems from this taboo.

The Rabbinic attitude is well summed up in the saying attributed to Rabbi Judah the Prince, 'in the name of the Band of Pious Men': 'Get you a handicraft as well as the Torah, for this is the meaning of "live joyfully with the wife whom thou lovest".' In their *Rabbinic Anthology* Montefiore and Loewe quote this dictum and explain: 'The wife must here be understood to mean the Torah.' [1] In the same way as we have come to reconsider the mystical view of the *Shechinah* in the light of our new self-understanding, in which the feminine dimension of our existence is affirmed, we may now be able to revise the intellectual view of Torah as wife and, instead, see it as it is: not as a God-surrogate but on its intrinsic merits. In our new scheme of things, based on our present understanding of the sources of Judaism, it is God Himself who is the metaphoric 'husband', Israel the 'bride' and the Torah the love-letter between the Lover and His beloved. God has written the text; Israel responds by studying it and seeking to live by it. As liberally as we may wish to

[1] C. G. Montefiore and H. Loewe, *A Rabbinic Anthology* (JPSA, Philadelphia, 1960), p. 443 (extract 1231).

interpret the notion of God's 'writing' the Torah, and as much as we may have reasons to reject the fundamentalist interpretation of the Mosaic authorship of the Pentateuch, we may still recognize how powerful the love-letter image is. We repudiate every attempt to place the Torah where God should be, but recognize its intrinsic significance for us, both men and women. The Torah is not the Lover of Israel; that is God's unique place. But the Torah is the document that describes the love and specifies the obligations of both Lover and beloved.

The 'romantic' image of Torah as a love-letter that is being put forward here should be linked to the more sober view, also to be found in Rabbinic literature, of Torah as a marriage contract. Torah – in its dual image of teaching and law – comprises both. As Professor Jakob Petuchowski has put it:

> The Song of Songs is almost unanimously understood by the commentators of the Synagogue as an allegory describing the courtship of God and Israel, climaxing in the 'marriage ceremony' at Mount Sinai. It is, therefore, not strange that, continuing the same line of thought, there should be rabbinic references to the Torah in terms of the 'marriage contract' legalising that 'union'.[2]

Petuchowski then goes on to describe how relevant that image is in our own days. It reflects a living, open relationship in which that which happens between the efforts of man and the Word of God becomes real and true. Whenever the exponents of Torah felt secure and at home in the world, they promoted such openness. They encouraged study rather than decision-making and promoted the struggle rather than the conclusion that eliminated alternative interpretations. A marriage contract based on love and trust reflects the Prophetic dimension in Jewish existence, which is not only to be found in the Bible, but also in Pharisaic Judaism and in much of what is best in Jewish literature throughout the ages. The future of Judaism is bound up with a restatement of this perennial theme.

But over and above the Prophetic, there is also a Priestly

---

[2] Jakob J. Petuchowski, *Ever Since Sinai*, 3rd edn (B. Arbit Books, Milwaukee, 1979), p. 3.

dimension in Jewish life, and the two have existed side by side, in creative conflict, long after the last Prophet had died and the destruction of the Temple in Jerusalem had rendered the Priestly class obsolete. Ahad Ha-am recognized it and expressed it in terms of the tension between Priest and Prophet:

> The Prophet is essentially a one-sided man. A certain moral idea fills his whole being, masters his every feeling and sensation, engrosses his whole attention . . . It is otherwise with the Priest. He appears on the scene at a time when Prophecy has already succeeded in hewing out a path for its Idea; when that Idea has already had a certain effect on the trend of society, and has brought about a new harmony or balance between the different forces at work . . . Not what *ought* to be, but what *can* be, is what he seeks.[3]

In our time the Prophetic–Pharisaic ideal of study has been largely supplanted by the Priestly–Rabbinic notion of law and observance. The marriage document has become petrified. What was intended as a dialectical relationship in which the realism of the Priest could prevent the Prophetic from degenerating into the esoteric, has in our days been reduced to a pedestrian realism being elevated to the normative. Strict adherence to the letter in place of a dialogue with the spirit is being advocated as a tool in the struggle for survival. Once again, in the name of Jewish survival, both education and observance are being trivialized and the open dialogue between the Message and the student petrified. The marriage contract has lost its dimension of love-letter and become a statute book.

To re-establish the tension between the *ought* and the *can*, between idealism and realism, is crucial in the effort to secure a future for Judaism. Torah, in the widest possible, as well as in the most narrow, sense of the word is a balance between love and law. It teaches both 'Love your neighbour as yourself' (*Leviticus* 19:18) and 'These are the commandments and regulations that the Lord enjoined upon the Israelites' (*Numbers* 36:13). The conventional Christian separation between

---

[3] Ahad Ha-am, *Selected Essays*, translated and edited by Leon Simon (JPSA, Philadelphia, 1962), p. 130f.

love and law, claiming a franchise on the former and burdening Judaism with the latter, is a vile distortion of the truth, but we Jews must make sure that we do not collude in it. We must instead affirm the Torah as both love-letter and marriage document.

Love, defined by Buber as the responsibility of the *I* for the *thou*, can never exist in its purity, on its own. Buber recognizes that it is inherent in the human situation that every *I–thou* deteriorates into an *I–it*: the immediate encounter between two subjects, in this case the living word of God and the eager student, sooner or later becomes a relationship between subject and object: the student classifies, generalizes, fixes rules. Deplorable though that may be in Buber's eyes, it is inevitable in our lives. We resign ourselves to the fact that the initial way in which Israel addresses the Eternal Thou becomes frozen into *it*: law, dogma, etc. The love-letter must become also a marriage contract. But when the multiplicity of regulations in that contract totally obscures the dimension of love, the future of Israel – the people, the faith and the land – is in danger. Our indictment of contemporary Jewish Orthodoxy is that it has petrified Torah into petty legalism, turned the sublime love-letter into an irrelevant printed card of a kind that those who are indifferent to each other exchange for the sake of civility. In the same way as Reform has tended to equate God with Jewish ethics, Orthodoxy has tended to equate Torah with legalism. When its upholders today kiss, cuddle and dance with the Torah they are holding a lifeless, heavy monolith. As it gets heavier and they get weaker, it is in danger of falling from their hands and shattering into a thousand pieces, like Moses' first tablets. Once again, those who most ardently seek to preserve it in order to survive are achieving the very opposite of what they mean to do.

To keep the Torah soft and supple and light it cannot be left in the sole custody of today's heirs of the ancient Priests. The responsibility must be shared by those who wish to follow in the footsteps of the Prophets. We must bear in mind that, in the final resort, legalism did not carry the day, even in the 'dark ages' in our history. The Temple and the Priesthood vanished; the message of the Prophets survived, even in the face of the claims of the early Christians (who mistook Apocalypse for Prophecy). Our task is to make it live now, not just as a lofty idea but as a practical programme, specifically in the realm of Jewish education and Jewish observance. Both should reflect the tension between love and obligation inherent in the Torah and manifest in the tension between Prophet and Priest.

Our task is complicated by the domination of secularism, which, as has been suggested earlier, is not merely an external force which threatens the world of religion but an insidious worm in the fabric of religion itself. In our secularized age the tension between Priestly 'realism' and Prophetic 'idealism' is not in the centre of Jewish life. It has been replaced by a secular indifference to both. Legalistic intransigence is in vogue not so much because Prophets have been muzzled but because the noise that religious extremists make is amplified by the silence of the masses. However, those who are indifferent to religion prefer religionists to be obscurantists in order to legitimize the secularists' lack of interest in what appears to them as 'the fringe'. Prophetic pathos has been smothered not only by Priestly legalism but also by secularist apathy, which at best, views Judaism only as a subject of academic interest, not as a living force.

The obstacles which prevent us from viewing the Torah as a love-letter *cum* marriage contract are formidable: the tendency in tradition to elevate it to an almost mystic entity – the bride only permitted to male Jews in search of the transcendental; the propensity, particularly in Orthodoxy, to limit it to a set of fixed rules, a body of teachings reduced to a code of law; the secularist fashion to render it obsolete and irrelevant. Since the future of Judaism is inseparable from the centrality of Torah, our concern for Jewish purpose prompts us to look at the whole body of Jewish teaching in its true light, i.e. as the product of the tension between the Prophetic and the Priestly, and to remove the obstacles that blur our vision. A new perspective on Jewish education and Jewish observance, both manifestations of Torah in our time, is a practical application of this our resolve.

18

Education or Training: Being versus Having

The tension between Prophet and Priest is reflected, *inter alia*, in the refusal of Jewish tradition to resolve the dichotomy between learning and doing. If the latter takes precedence it is, in the last resort, not as a goal in itself but as a way to learning. Similarly, study which does not lead to action is barren and can be discounted. Judaism is the outcome of the dialectical relationship between the two and our critique of contemporary Judaism rests partly on the observation that that relationship has been broken: Jews have fled either into academia, 'education and culture', or they have sought refuge in behaviourist observance. This has made secular Judaism barren and Orthodox Judaism blind. The fact that both the barrenness and the blindness have been elevated into 'tools of Jewish survival' has made it very difficult to be critical of them; that is why, for example, both secular Israeli education and Orthodox conformism have had such a sway over Jewish life.

Nevertheless, an attempt to describe the future of Judaism from the Prophetic perspective must go beyond both secularism and Orthodoxy and reaffirm the tension between the Priest and the Prophet. Education and observance have to reflect this. The separate compartments in which these exist have to be dismantled in favour of an integrated programme. The division between those who teach and those who do is inimical both to the teaching and the doing. Torah means both. To separate the one from the other is to falsify the love-letter and the marriage contract. Inevitably, in an attempt to point to the possible direction of Jewish education we must be critical of its present course, for behind the polarization into learning and doing there is a fundamental *malaise*.

Erich Fromm, basing himself on his understanding of Torah, expresses the *malaise* as the desire to replace *being* with *having*. In its traditional setting, Torah is a way of being. The student who relates to it becomes himself in the process of study and, at the same time, as it were, makes it real. It is the *I-thou* relationship between the lover and the message of his beloved, which makes that message alive and full of new nuances and meanings each time he reads it. That relationship deteriorates easily into an *I-it* relationship when the latter becomes a dead object, which no longer affirms me but gives me power because I have it. Starting off from his Jewish roots, Fromm recognizes a universal pattern:

> The difference between the mode of having and the mode of being in the sphere of *knowing* is expressed in two formulations: 'I have knowledge' and 'I know'. *Having* knowledge is taking and keeping possession of available knowledge (information); *knowing* is functional and part of the process of productive thinking.[1]

The desire to *have* knowledge rather than to *know* is, according to Fromm, a function of the craving for power and as such an expression of real insecurity. The Jewish world, threatened to its very core by the Holocaust, came to cling to this kind of knowledge in the mistaken belief that it would guarantee its survival. As a result it created a host of institutions which illustrate Fromm's description of the ills of modern education:

> Our education generally tries to train people to *have* knowledge as a possession, by and large commensurate with the amount of property or social prestige they are likely to have in later life. The minimum they receive is the amount they will need in order to function properly in their work. In addition they are each given a 'luxury-knowledge package' to enhance their feeling of worth, the size of each such package being in accord with the person's probable social prestige. The schools are the factories in which these overall knowledge packages are produced.[2]

The criticism that Fromm levels against all institutions of

---

[1] Erich Fromm, *To Have or to Be?* (Jonathan Cape 1978), p. 39.
[2] ibid., p. 41.

learning is, alas, also applicable to the Jewish ones, not least Jewish Day Schools. There is no indication that the mere imparting of knowledge, however intensively done, makes for Jewish commitment. For that more is required: the cognitive and the affective dimension of Torah, learning and doing, must be re-integrated. This may be possible in some cases by drastically reforming existing establishments but, more likely, new ways of imparting Judaism will have to evolve. These would be based on the fact that it is the development of a child's sense of wonder, not his accumulation of facts, that encourages him to *know* (not merely to *have* knowledge) and to seek the source of that knowledge, God.

And yet, it would be unfair to ignore the significance of the Day Schools in contemporary Judaism. The Hebrew word for education is *chinuch*. It means 'dedication' and reflects a total commitment, unlike training which only leads to skills. These Day Schools try to provide it. The Zionist movement and Orthodoxy have attempted to create an integrated Jewish educational system. It may not be as satisfactory as we would like it, but it is a serious and credible endeavour. Reform, by contrast, is in this respect far behind. Only in the last few years have non-Orthodox religious Day Schools begun to emerge, but the vast majority of Reform Jews are still hostile to segregation in education and still cling to the belief that by creating separate Day Schools we provoke anti-Semitism. There is, of course, no evidence of that. There appears to be very little that Jews can do, or refrain from doing, to please anti-Semites. The reluctance to send children to Jewish Schools has little to do with the desire to protect them from enemies and much with the wish to bar their access to Jewish commitment; it is an assimilationist ploy.

The future of Jewish education rests on a school system in which learning and living are one. One way would be to provide residential schools. Concerned parents, having recognized their failure to establish a Jewish home, would then be able to provide a suitable milieu for their children. However, financial and other considerations make this impossible; the only Jewish boarding school in Britain is also the most expensive one in the country. Day Schools are, however, a workable compromise, if they are run by men and women imbued with the kind of vision described here.

Full-time education in Jewish Day Schools, highly desirable though it is, is not the only way in which Jews can be educated along the lines suggested here. The importance of the Synagogue as an educational institution should not be underestimated. Since over half of Diaspora Jewry in the English-speaking world is attached to congregations that are grouped around Synagogues, it has great potential. The potential is not being realized for the same reasons that the opportunities for full-time education are being squandered.

The Synagogue Sunday School as it now exists, whether or not augmented by Hebrew classes during the week, is a failure. It brings together, with the help of parental coercion, tired and confused youngsters for brief episodes of Jewish study and fragments of Jewish living. It creates in the minds of the children a suspicion of and a disdain for Judaism, because what is being taught on Sundays has no relevance for the rest of the week and, therefore, there seems to be no point in learning it. The argument in favour of such part-time Jewish education has been that it promotes, at least, Jewish survival and is therefore better than no education at all. In order to promote viable alternatives in Jewish education we should question this assumption. The absence of the Sunday School may remove the sense of being imposed upon which the Jewish child carries into adulthood and which prompts him to deny his Judaism in later life. Such absence may, moreover, force parents to seek more viable ways of giving their children a Jewish education, e.g. through the camps referred to below. Finally, if the Sunday School were to disappear, a tool in the service of secularization would perhaps have been removed.

For the secular temper which pervades Diaspora Jewry has turned the Synagogue into a *Barmitsvah* factory: every boy must *have* a *Barmitsvah* (not *be Barmitsvah!*); the reasons for this have been considered earlier. The fact that the celebration is linked with getting presents further stresses its materialist nature. As a result, only such learning as is conducive to a creditable performance in Synagogue is being sought. In this scheme of things there is no room for a dialogue with the living Torah. Girls are, of course, ignored since they are outside the *Barmitsvah* orbit. In some congregations equivalent ceremonies for girls have been established but, again, not to provide true education for them, but to train them to perform at some ceremony.

The Orthodox Synagogue is, by and large, content with the system, because it likes to impart rules, almost irrespective of whether its nominal adherents are likely to carry them out or not. Those truly committed, it is expected, will send their children to Day Schools, but the secularized members tend to collude with the establishment in 'putting on a show' instead of practising *chinuch* in the full sense of the word.

In theory, Reform and Conservative Synagogues are different. But since they, particularly the former, have a minimalist–universalist vision of Jewish education, they do not seem to have been able to provide the *milieu* conducive to *chinuch*. Instead, the same pressures on *Barmitsvah* and performance have been allowed to pervade. Even the fact that many such Synagogues now provide equal opportunities for both boys and girls does not really ameliorate the situation, for true education continues to be neglected whereas superficial training is being promoted.

The two religious manifestations of contemporary Judaism – Orthodoxy and Reform – as well as their non-religious sister, Zionism, recognize that they have failed and seek to do something about it. The most imaginative and effective efforts concentrate around camps and residential courses. For it is generally recognized that the Jewish home has not been able to provide the atmosphere conducive to Jewish learning and Jewish life. Therefore, both children and adults can be fired with a love of Judaism through the experience of a few weeks in a Jewish atmosphere. Such camps and institutes are particularly successful when conducted in Israel. By combining the need for recreation and leisure, with the opportunity for education and learning, we may be able to achieve that which neither the school nor the Synagogue has so far been able to bring about.

The residential camp, or course, or institute is the only way in which true dialogue – with fellow campers or students as well as with the Torah taught – becomes possible and realizable in the actual activities of the group. Moreover, potentially it could break down barriers between the various denominations, since the life of a collective demands an eclectic, not a doctrinaire, approach. It is, therefore, not surprising that it is Conservative Judaism in America – with its mixture of traditionalism, modernity and nationalism – that has been the most successful sponsor of such camps. If Jews in the West cannot lead a Jewish life 24 hours a day, seven days a week, 52 weeks in the year, they may at least be able to do so for 24 hours a day fourteen or twenty-one days a year. The fact that more and more of us are getting longer holidays would make this kind of Jewish activity possible. It could be further augmented by weekends away and preparation sessions in-between.

Residential facilities, taking advantage of the ever-growing opportunities for leisure that Western society makes available, should not be considered for children and youth only, for they are equally suitable for adults. To be able to share one's thoughts on God, Torah and Israel with fellow Jews, to be taught by distinguished teachers and to be given the opportunity to experience Judaism in practice is attractive to young and old alike, as the achievements of the Brandeis Institute in California suggest. The common experience of a few days together forges bonds of friendship between participants which they in turn strengthen by attending together weekly adult education programmes and other activities in their communities. Such involvement also eases the pressure on the middle-class family by offering an extended family surrogate. What is as yet quite unique in California could soon become commonplace in many places, Jewish and non-Jewish alike.

Chavurot[3] (fellowships) should also be considered as forerunners to this vision of Jewish education of tomorrow. They came into being as a response to the need for the cognitive and the affective dimensions of Torah to come together, both in residential settings and through regular occasional meetings, particularly in connection with the celebration of Sabbaths and Festivals. Groups of like-minded Jews emerged in many Jewish centres, particularly in the United States. The very existence of these groups points to new dimensions in Jewish education. The *chavurah* movement may be regarded as a forerunner to the 'Leisure and Learning' schemes envis-

---

[3] For explanation see Glossary: the movement owes much to the writings of Jacob Neusner. See, e.g., his *Fellowship in Judaism* (Vallentine Mitchell 1963) and his *Judaism in the Secular Age* (Vallentine Mitchell 1970).

aged here. Whether the conventional synagogue or independent bodies should promote such schemes may depend on circumstances. Both alternatives have advantages, and both are full of pitfalls, for they can easily be 'hi-jacked' by commercial enterprises or ideological movements which will use the new institutions for their own ends, and in no way offer the participants an opportunity to *be* Jews. At its best, this movement that combines study with practice should be viewed in the context of the new opportunities for leisure and the quest for purpose that such increased leisure awakens. Torah has always been the antidote to boredom in Jewish life. In today's world it may turn out to be in greater demand than ever before.

All this is not to say that, by taking Jews out of their ordinary *milieu* of *having* into a few days' of Jewish *being*, we will have solved all the problems of Jewish education. In fact, we may be creating new ones, particularly through the 'bifurcation' between the secular world and the 'pure' spiritual world. What set out to be a way of offering integrated Jewish education may turn out to be a method of providing a type of retreat which is consistent with the Christian division between the Church and the world but inimical to Jewish teaching. The irony of that possibility should not escape us. Nevertheless we may be prepared to take the risk because, for all their theological purity, the existing Jewish educational institutions are not achieving what is necessary for a Jewish future.

The above reflections prompt two further considerations before we turn to the other aspect of Torah, observance: firstly, the question of the use of leisure and, secondly, the future of the Jewish home. These digressions will enable us to pay some attention to the universalist dimension of Torah before we return to consider its particularist manifestation.

19

Work and Worship

A verse in the Book of *Joshua* (1:8) reads: 'Let not this Book of the Teaching cease from your lips, but recite it day and night, so that you may observe faithfully all that is written in it. Only then will you prosper in your undertakings and only then will you be successful.' Holy study, which in Jewish tradition is the highest form of worship, is, according to this verse, to be the sole occupation of the pious: 'Let not this book of the Teaching cease from your lips, but recite it day and night.' However, *Deuteronomy* 11:13–14 states: 'If, then, you obey the commandments that I enjoin upon you this day, loving the Lord your God and serving Him with all your heart and soul, I will grant the rain for your land in season, the early rain and the late. You shall gather in your new grain and wine and oil etc.' The Talmud[1] now asks: if I am to study day and night – when am I to gather in the grain and the wine and the oil? If worship is to be my sole occupation – when am I to work in order to provide for myself and my family?

Rabbi Ishmael, who lived in the second century CE and was of a practical bent, suggests that both Biblical verses are deliberately given so that we may balance the one with the other. If we only had the passage in *Deuteronomy*, we might not work for the Lord through study and worship. Therefore, both are necessary; between them they give us the truth for, far from cancelling each other out, they complement each other. But Rabbi Shimon bar Yochai, Ishmael's contemporary and a mystic, disagrees. He is quoted as having taught that if 'a man ploughs at the time for ploughing, and he sows at the time for sowing, and he harvests at the time for harvesting, and he threshes at the time for threshing, and he winnows in

[1] *Berachot* 35b.

the time of wind – the Teaching, what will become of it? Rather when Israel does the will of God, their work is done by others . . . and when Israel does not do the will of God, their work is done by them . . . and not only so, but the work of others will be done by them.' This mystic, then, sees work and worship as being mutually exclusive and has no difficulties in taking sides.

Normative Judaism, refused to accept the mystical view and again and again sought to reinforce Rabbi Ishmael's practical and balanced opinion. Thus the same Talmud passage quotes a later authority validating the down-to-earth position on the basis that experience has proved it to be successful, whereas the mystical approach had failed. There is also a story told of Rava, the great Jewish teacher in Babylonia in the third century, that he implored his disciples not to come and study with him at harvest time, but work in the fields instead, 'so that you may not be in trouble over your food throughout the year'.

The identification of worship with study has continued throughout Jewish history until this very day. But periodically movements have arisen which, initially at least, rebelled against the excessive intellectualism which this approach bred. The best known of these movements – largely thanks to the writings of Martin Buber – is Chasidism. Chasidism started in Eastern Europe in the second half of the eighteenth century and has many adherents, plus many more admirers, to this very day. The same tension between work and worship remains, but it is now expressed in another story, reflecting the very different setting of Chasidism compared to the world of the Talmud.

A man was once rebuked by his neighbours for being in a prayer shawl and phylacteries – the outer manifestations of Jewish worship – while oiling the wheels of his cart. 'Look' they said, 'he oils his wheels while he prays.' But their teacher, the Chasidic master, told them that they totally misunderstood the situation. He praised the man and said 'O Lord, what a holy people! Even when they oil the wheels of their wagons they pray unto You!

Both the Chasidic master and the Talmudic sage were articulating an important tenet in Judaism, reflected in the

Hebrew language itself which has the same word for 'work' and for 'worship' – *avodah*, best translated as 'service', a term which points to both aspects. Since Jewish tradition and theology do not know the distinction between sacred and secular, but believe that all aspects of reality are potentially holy – and it is man's task to make the potential actual through the act of sanctification – no sharp distinction need be made between worship and the rest of life, or work and the rest of life.

Equating work with worship is, by implication, taking issue with Josef Pieper, the Austrian philosopher, who has written that 'culture depends for its very existence on leisure, and leisure, in its turn, is not possible unless it has a durable and consequently living link with the *cultus*, with divine worship'.[2] Pieper identifies worship with leisure, not with work, and to make his point he is even prepared to tamper with the translation of *Psalm* 46:11, which clearly means, 'Be still [or possibly 'desist' or 'let be'] and know that I am God,' by rendering it, 'Have leisure and know that I am God'.[3]

How alien Pieper's view is to the Jewish mind is shown in Norman Lamm's critique of the use of leisure in American society: 'Leisure is gradually replacing work as the best of culture.'[4] Lamm follows here the line of the Dutch historian Johan Huizinga who has written that 'culture arises in the form of play', but that later 'the play-element gradually recedes into the background, being absorbed for the most part in the sacred sphere'.[5] Lamm is critical of his own society precisely because it appears to have regressed from worship to play at the same time as those living in that society have more and more time away from work.

Jewish tradition does not regard work *per se* as being fundamental to human existence. Despite the quip that it is the Jews who have invented the Protestant work ethic, and notwithstanding hard-working Jewish immigrants and children of immigrants in Britain, in the United States and elsewhere, theologically, work is never regarded as more than a necessity. It is never an autonomous virtue the way study and prayer are. But to be able to study and to pray in peace and dignity

[2] Josef Pieper, *Leisure the Basis of Culture*, (Collins 1965), p. 17.
[3] ibid., p. 20.
[4] Norman Lamm, *Faith and Doubt* (Ktav, New York, 1971), p. 187.
[5] Johan Huizinga, *Homo Ludens* (Paladin 1970), p. 66f.

we have to work to earn a living. To combine both worship
and work is a formula for happiness. Although the Bible
commands, 'Six days you shall labour and do all your work'
(*Exodus* 20:9), it is what follows that really matters: 'but the
seventh day is a Sabbath of the Lord your God' (*Exodus*
20:10). Jewish tradition exhorts its adherents to observe the
Sabbath much more than it urges them to work on the remaining six days. However, it also recognizes that without
working to provide throughout the week there will not be
much opportunity to celebrate and observe the Sabbath. To
extend the Sabbath beyond the twenty-four hours or so that
it lasts by devoting more time to its pursuits and less time to
the wear and tear of labour is not sinful, but it may be
impractical.

At this stage it may be legitimate to reflect on the place of
the Sabbath in the Jewish scheme of things. It is to be a day
of cessation from labour – but not a day of leisure in the
current, play, sense of the word. You work on the Sabbath,
too – but not to earn a living; you work in the service of God.
You are commanded to refrain from all manner of work which
leads to *having* things so that you can work at *being* in the
presence of God. That latter work is prayer and study. Lamm,
points out that Jewish liturgy regards the term for Sabbath
rest, *menuchah*, as a form of work – divine service – which,
incidentally, the Jew is duty bound to share with all mankind.

> The prohibition of labour [on the Sabbath] implies the
> cessation of our activities imposed by us as creative person-
> alities upon the natural world. But authentic *menuhah* [Sab-
> bath rest] requires that on the Sabbath we direct these
> creative changes not onto nature but onto ourselves, spiri-
> tually and intellectually. *Menuhah* is not a suspension, for
> one day of the week, of our creative energies, but a refo-
> cusing of our creative talents upon ourselves. The difference
> between the prohibited *melakhah* [work] and the recom-
> mended *menuhah* [rest] lies not in the *fact of* creativity, but
> in the *object* of one's creative powers . . .[6]

Work need not be something separate from rest. The two
can co-exist and be blended according to the needs and re-

---

[6] Lamm, op. cit., p. 198f.

quirements of any particular epoch in history. With less need to work for a living, which appears to be the formula for the future, there is greater opportunity to work for the glory of God; with less need for six days' labour, there is more scope for several days of Sabbath. And in case we suspect that this would only be regarded as an advantage by the pious and the learned, Jewish tradition insists that it is the Sabbath *activity* that matters, not the level of sophistication. With all its intellectualism, Judaism has never excluded the less endowed and the less educated; it has only castigated him who refuses to try, not the person who does not achieve spectacular results.

It is essential that everybody tries because the Sabbath is seen as a foretaste of the Messianic era. The longer the Sabbath lasts the closer we come to the ideal future. When the Jew recites his grace after meals on the Sabbath he adds a special prayer, anticipating 'a day that shall be wholly a Sabbath and rest in life everlasting'. The Sabbath is the seventh day, the culmination of the working week and the ultimate purpose of that week – unlike Sunday, which is seen as the beginning of a new week – in the same way as the Messianic future is not a new beginning but the culmination and the consummation of the, as yet unredeemed, present. Labour is a means to an end, not an end in itself. Modernity with its shorter working hours reduces the time we need to spend on the means and allows more time for the end. As such it has Messianic potential.

In the same way as nobody needs to feel excluded from the activity that is Sabbath rest, however humble and uneducated, so no form of honourable work is to be looked down upon. There is, for example, no loss of status in manual labour. In fact, most of the sages of the Talmud and even more the masters of Chasidism, had what today would be called humble occupations. Precisely because work as such is not the centre of human existence, but only a necessary pre-requisite, every honest form of earning a living is acceptable. Everything that prevents my family and me from starving and begging and is legal is also honourable. It is only those who live to work, rather than work to live, who are snobbish or status-seeking about their jobs.

Idleness, on the other hand, is totally reprehensible, because there is never need for redundancy in the realm of study and prayer, which is the real purpose of human existence. God, the creator, revealed His Teaching to His creatures that they should study it and thus know His will. Such study and observance – worship in the widest sense of the word – makes Redemption possible. The individual who works in order to have the means to worship helps to consummate the purpose of Creation in Revelation. By being idle he slows down the process and so stands against God in a kind of passive resistance.

Like everything else, the Nazis sought to invalidate this idea by the cynical inscription over the gate to the death camp at Auschwitz: 'Arbeit macht frei' (work makes you free). The murderous cynicism behind that slogan is powerfully described by a survivor, Eugene Heimler:

> One day the commandant of the camp decided, on the advice of SS 'medical experts', to do an 'experiment in mental health'. He ordered a few hundred of us to move sand from one end of the factory to another, and when we had completed this task we were ordered to move it back to the original place. At first we thought that our guards must have made a mistake, but it soon became clear that they had not. From then on, day after day, week after week, we had to carry the sand to and fro, until gradually people's minds began to give way. Even those who had been working steadily in the factory before . . . were affected, for the work had some use and purpose, even if it was for the Germans, but in the face of a completely meaningless task people started to lose their sanity.

Heimler adds: 'My comrades had died not at the hands of the Gestapo, but because they had nothing to live for and had been forced to do futile acts which killed their spirit.'[7] Perpetual bondage is hell, for killing time kills people. Heimler's description of his camp experience is to be found in his book on social work in the chapter on the so-called Hendon experiment which led him, in due course, to formulate a scale of social functioning and now to occupy a special chair at the University of Calgary in Canada. Heimler has formulated his credo as a social worker in terms of his experience as a con-

[7] Eugene Heimler, *Mental Illness and Social Work* (Penguin 1967), p. 107f.

centration camp inmate: 'If purposeless tasks can destroy
people's will to survive, what could purposeful tasks do for
them, even for those to whom early satisfactions had been
denied?' [8] he asks.

Heimler is by no means the only camp survivor who has
dedicated his life to the kind of therapy that helps people to
function better at work. Two other names spring to mind:
Viktor Frankl and Bruno Bettelheim. Their quest for meaningful occupation, for real freedom, as a reaction to the experience of total bondage and absolute meaninglessness of the
camp has come to embody some of the ideas alluded to so far.
Similarly Erich Fromm, in his quest for freedom as *being*
rather than *having*, builds on his experience of the Nazi regime
as he knew it before leaving his native Germany, and frequently links it to his Jewish roots.

Bruno Bettelheim, in his book *The Informed Heart*, tells in
great detail how the Nazis reduced the Jews to machines by
taking away their purpose in life, and Viktor Frankl, in his
system of therapy which he calls 'logotherapy', shows how
man can regain that purpose. Both point to the real danger of
bondage and slavery and thus, in this respect, speak not only
the same language as Erich Fromm, but also the language of
the Hebrew Bible. Again and again does Moses say to Phar-
oah, 'Let my people go!', but almost invariably the next word,
spoken in the name of God, is *v'ya-avduni* (from that word
avodah which means both 'worship' and 'work') 'that they
may serve Me' (e.g. *Exodus* 7:26). Freedom has a purpose –
to serve God. Similarly, the Israelite may not sell himself, or
be sold, into permanent servitude, 'for they are My servants,
whom I freed from the land of Egypt' (*Leviticus* 25:42), and,
as if to stress the point, a few verses later in the same chapter:
'For it is to Me that the Israelites are servants: they are My
servants, whom I freed from the land of Egypt, I the Lord
your God' (*Leviticus* 25:55). Service to God demands freedom
from man. The redemption that the Exodus initiates makes
such freedom a theological necessity. The Nazis knew it and
so deprived the Jews of it before killing them. Some of those
who survived are now dedicated to the promotion of the
freedom that makes for *avodah*, service.

[8] ibid., p. 108.

Bondage, total immersion in work, whether voluntary or compulsory that has no room for the Sabbath, makes worship, service, impossible. Thus when Moses carried the message of redemption to his own people, they were not able to receive it: 'When Moses told this to the Israelites, they would not listen to Moses, their spirits crushed by cruel bondage' (*Exodus* 6:9). Pieper comes to a similar conclusion when, with obvious reference to Marxism, he writes: 'If the essence of "proletarian" is the fact of being fettered to the process of work, then the central problem of liberating men from this condition lies in making a whole field of significant activity available and open to the working man.' Pieper, in response to Marxism, insists that 'this end cannot be attained by purely political measures and by widening . . . the life of the individual economically', but by teaching man to 'occupy his leisure' or 'work his leisure'.[9] Work in its proper context is a tool in man's quest for freedom, not a means of depriving man of freedom. Jewish teaching throughout the ages points to the former, Jewish experience in modern times offers evidence of the latter.

Such references to what is specifically Jewish enable us to make some comments about the general. The first observation is this: since work is only a means to an end, not an end in itself, it must have purpose. Heimler suggests that even destructive purpose is better than no purpose at all. Work that is, or appears to be, meaningless is by definition destructive; it drives you mad. Viewed in this light, automation that enables machines to take over the chores of men should be welcomed and encouraged. It sets men free and works for their sanity and mental balance; it is the very antithesis and negation of that slogan over the gate at Auschwitz. Of course, there may be economic and political reasons why automation should be resisted, but not on theological grounds. A television programme on robots some time ago closed with the words: 'When robots do the work we will be able to do what we want to do, not what we've got to do.' That is real freedom; it exposes the cynicism of the Nazis who tried to reduce men to robots. In the same TV programme, another participant remarked that Orwell's *1984* does not speak of robots precisely

[9] Pieper, op. cit., p. 57f.

because, in the book, man is depicted as a robot. Automation, then, enables man to escape the fate described by Orwell and remain human even in 1984 and beyond.

Pieper, the philosopher steeped in classical scholarship, reminds his readers that the Greek for 'leisure', *skole*, is the same as the English 'school',[10] and he quotes Aristotle approvingly: 'That is the principal point: with what kind of activity is man to occupy his leisure.'[11] The Jewish answer is simple: through worship and, more specifically, through the kind of worship that is manifest in holy study. The fact that man has now more leisure gives him unique opportunities to devote more of his time to God and thus hasten the redemption. Absence of work makes the Messianic future possible when 'teaching shall come forth from Zion', and 'every man shall sit under his grapevine or fig tree with no one to disturb him' (*Micah* 4:2 and 4).

A newspaper report[12] on Professor Tom Stonier's working paper to the Government Think Tank, states: 'In a concluding comment, Professor Stonier says it must become the priority of government, industry and the trade unions to effect the orderly transfer of labour from the manufacturing to the knowledge industries. The logical way to accomplish this is by means of huge expansion in the education system.' It is a response that could have come from Jewish tradition. However, I cannot see the kind of education that we need coming from 'government, industry and the trade unions', but from Church and Synagogue, Mosque and Temple. For these are depositories of wisdom that makes for *being* rather than *having*, since the latter leads to more labour and less freedom. It is only the agencies of established religion that could, so it seems, respond to the late E. F. Schumacher's call for education to be 'first and foremost, the transmission of ideas of value, of what to do with our lives', since in his view, 'more education can help us only if it produces more wisdom'.[13] To recognize not only the theological dimension of the issue before us but also of the religious responsibility to tackle the problem is, a matter of urgency. The vision of the future in

[10] ibid., p. 21.
[11] ibid., p. 58.
[12] *The Times*, 13 November 1978.
[13] E. F. Schumacher, *Small Is Beautiful* (Abacus 1974), p. 66.

which Torah as worship and as an alternative to labour dominates, not only the Jewish world but society at large, depends on how we discharge that responsibility.

The Synagogue and the Church must be judged in terms of their sense of urgency and responsibility. The primary task of a rabbi is to be a teacher and I understand this to include being a facilitator who enables people to free themselves, even if only a little, from *having*, to enter the realm of *being*, not by denying materialism but by using it for non-material ends and by devoting their energies to worship, not only to work. Perhaps the Christian clergyman can join in this enterprise. The common theological basis of priest and rabbi might help individuals to sanctify time rather than kill it. Edmond Fleg has written that he is a Jew 'because, for Israel, the world is not yet completed: men are completing it'.[14] There need not be anything specifically Jewish about that. Thomas Merton writes about the same thing, when he explains that *being* is more than what Eastern religions teach. He writes:

> Our vocation is not simply to *be*, but to work together with God in the creation of our own life, our own identity, our own destiny . . . We do not know clearly beforehand what the results of this work will be. The secret of my full identity is hidden in Him. He alone can make me who I am, or rather who I will be when at last I fully begin to be. But unless I desire this identity and work to find it with Him and in Him, the work will never be done.[15]

[14] Edmond Fleg, *Why I am a Jew* (Gollancz 1943), p. 61.
[15] Quoted in Anne Bancroft, *Modern Mystics and Sages* (Paladin 1978), p. 26.

20

Coming Home

The stress on education in residential settings and the argument in favour of the Synagogue and the community as the
vehicles through which Torah can be transmitted to those
who seek to fill their increased leisure with meaning, both
imply a recognition of the demise of the Jewish home and the
weakening of the family as carriers of Torah and values where
being precedes *having*. It will be argued here that this is only
a temporary state of affairs. The Jewish home may have been
weakened but it has not been destroyed. There is every reason
why we should keep as much as possible of the remaining
structure, for we will have to rebuild it in response to changed
external circumstances. And what once seemed uniquely, or
principally, Jewish may soon become universally Western.

The present crisis of the family stems from a number of
factors, some transient, others irreversible. To the latter category belong phenomena such as a new understanding of the
role of women, the availability of contraceptives, the increased
level of education, including access to psychological insights,
the claim to the right for happiness and personal fulfilment
and many others. There are also factors, however, which
currently seem to threaten the home and the family, but
which may very well no longer apply by the end of this
century. Chiefly among these is probably the change in the
way people communicate with each other.

At present, much time is spent in travelling to and from
work, including working abroad, as well as travelling in pursuit of leisure, be it to the weekend cottage or the summer
holiday. The increase in the price of oil and the scarcity of
that commodity, coupled with ever-growing availability of
telephones, computers and similar technological inventions
will make it both necessary and possible to work at home and

from home and to communicate with others televisually. We
will be forced to spend much more time at home than we are
doing now and we will depend on each other to make our life
and leisure at home as varied and as enjoyable as possible. We
have suggested that the Synagogue and the Church as community centres may come into their own. Let us now look at
the potential and the prospect of the home, viewed here from
the perspective of Jewish tradition.

There is no need to view the Synagogue and the home as
being in conflict with one another, even when the former
appears to take on some of the functions of the latter. Home
observance and home traditions have always depended on
models: mothers teaching daughters, fathers instructing sons.
The shock of emancipation broke the chain, for the gulf
between parents and children came to span centuries when in
one move from Poland or Russia to Western Europe or the
United States, lasting perhaps only a few weeks, Jews stepped
out of the Middle Ages into the twentieth century. Modern
Jews could not model themselves on their predecessors, even
when they wanted to retain some measure of home life and
home observance. As a result, they either just 'went through
the motions', in a dull and joyless manner, or they romanti-
cized the past and thus removed it from the realm of reality.
The Synagogue, therefore, has had to become a home substitute in order to show how tradition can be combined with
joy. The stress on residential camps and weekends is an
expression of that need. It is an emergency measure rather
than an alternative life style. The creative tension between the
community and the home that has always characterized Jewish
life can be maintained to enrich individuals in the future as
it has in the past.

As the importance of the home is emphasized again, the
necessity to translate the observance of the community into
the home will also become apparent. The community's role
as a model for individual behaviour will be stressed, as will
the opportunities for education outside the conventional
framework of school and university. The increased availability
of leisure gives us new access to study. The availability of
technological aids makes such study possible at home. The
use of modern techniques could make studying both effective
and enjoyable. Jewish education must take advantage of these

opportunities. We may not be able to take many Jews to *Yeshivot*, but we may bring the greatest scholars of these and all other kinds of Jewish institutions of learning to the video screen in every home. What the Open University in Britain has pioneered can be adapted and used in a much wider context.

The vision of a home-centred life, sustained to a large extent by novel means of communication, in which the traditional Jewish values of home observance and *talmud torah* can again come to the fore, will, however, only be possible if we come to terms with the implications of the sexual revolution. The reality of equality between the sexes and the availability of contraceptives are two of the factors which have contributed to the drastic revision of sexual mores. The 'new morality' is inimical to the Jewish home. If the home is to be affirmed and re-established a distinctly Jewish approach to sexuality is needed. Once again, non-Jews may wish to learn from it.

Judaism is not puritanical. It affirms sex not only as necessary for human reproduction but as a noble expression of love, care and responsibility. It is perhaps this that makes traditional Judaism so hostile to anything that seems to cheapen the gift of sex. Although it is difficult to defend a system so blatantly patriarchal in outlook and sexist in practice, the overall view of sexuality in Judaism is surprisingly 'modern' and humanistic compared with other religions. Judaism in no way denies sexuality, but it believes it to be legitimate only *within* marriage. Jewish law is lenient in its treatment of pre-marital sex, but it never encourages it: its stress on early marriages is its practical response to the young person's craving for sexual fulfilment. It is fierce in its condemnation of extra-marital sex. Within marriage, however, it regards sexuality as a unique opportunity for true happiness to both partners.

The technical term for the Jewish marriage ceremony is *kiddushin*. It comes from the Hebrew word *kadosh*, 'holy'. But *kadosh* also has the connotation 'to be set apart'. The married couple are set apart from everybody else when they are consecrated to each other. The act of consecration carries with it the responsibility of love and the hope of happiness. The married couple establish a sanctuary in which they are the priests, thus fulfilling the Biblical injunction, 'You shall be to

Me a kingdom of priests and a holy nation' (*Exodus* 19:6). The Temple has not been succeeded by the Synagogue but by the home; the home is for the Jew what the Church is for the Christian, a true successor to the Biblical sanctuary.

It is in this context that we must view not only the Prophetic use of marriage as the metaphor of the relationship between God and man but also Buber's understanding of marriage as the setting most conducive to real meeting between men and women, and between both and God. Ignaz Maybaum, for all his opposition to Buber, uses a similar theologic-social framework when he equates monotheism with monogamy and writes that 'with the insistence on monogamy we approach the very depth of religious life':

> Gifts donated to the Temple are, according to biblical law, consecrated, remain holy and are not to be exposed to profanation. Such consecration binds man and woman together in marriage, and their bond is an holy order. From out of a host of men and women two people are segregated from all other men and women and are consecrated to each other and dedicated to their sole companionship. Monogamy, like everything concerning the rules of the Temple worship, is not merely a social form of life, it is a holy order. Jewish–Christian monotheism, affirming the Oneness of God, demands a oneness which every married couple represents. Monogamy is like monotheism. Both exist through faithfulness to a unique oneness.[1]

Monogamy, however, need not be defended on theological grounds only. Thus George F. Gilder asserts that 'the widespread belief that monogamous marriage is obsolete is a grave portent for our society'.[2]

> Monogamy is central to any democratic social contract, designed to prevent a breakdown of society into 'war of every man against every other man'. In order to preserve order, a man may relinquish liberty, prosperity, and power to the state. But if he has to give up his wife to his boss, he is no longer a man. A society of open sexual competition,

[1] Ignaz Maybaum, *Happiness Outside the State* (Oriel, Stocksfield, 1980), p. 73.
[2] George F. Gilder, *Sexual Suicide* (Millington 1974), p. 46.

in which the rich and powerful – or even the sexually
attractive – can command large numbers of women is a
society with the most intolerable hierarchy of all. In any
polygamous society some men have no wives at all; denied
women and children, they are in effect deprived of the very
substance of life. Monogamy is egalitarianism in the realm
of love. It is a mode of rationing. It means – to put it
crudely – one to a customer. Competition is intense enough
even so, because of the sexual inequality of human beings.
But under a regime of monogamy there are limits.

Gilder's conclusion, therefore, has to be taken seriously:
'When the society stops enforcing monogamy, a social order
based on monogamous families will break down into a system
based on the bitter hierarchies of sexual power.' [3] It is not
unlike Maybaum's conclusion:

> . . . if today families do not remain what they were in the
> days of the biblical patriarchs, if families are consumed to
> be mere material for history, if families do not withstand
> the pressure of the permissive society, history decays, civi-
> lizations decline and die like plants without sun and water.
> Western man lives in history. But when he becomes a man
> of the mass age, when he becomes uprooted from the fam-
> ily, he has nothing to contribute to civilization.[4]

The above references make it clear that it is not only the
Jewish home that is being spoken of here, but the place of
the family in society as a whole. The equation of monotheism
with monogamy also offers a new realm of co-operation between the monotheistic religions in the face of secular per-
missiveness. Especially the two monotheistic religions now
firmly committed to monogamy, Christianity and Judaism,
have a particular responsibility to act as a corrective to the
society that seeks to break up the traditional family in order
to replace it with alternatives.

Attempts to destroy the family in pursuit of happiness are
doomed to fail. The kibbutz is a case in point. Its founders
were men and women who, under the influence of socialist

[3] George F. Gilder, 'The Defence of Monogamy', in *Commentary*, lviii, 5
(November 1974) pp. 31–6.
[4] Maybaum, op. cit., p. 72.

ideology, believed themselves to be unable to live within the confines of the Jewish home. Modelling themselves on the Chasidic gathering, when the disciples would assemble around their master, especially at festivals, they wanted to create a form of home life which would be free of possessions of any kind and free from the restraints of sexual fidelity. Economically the kibbutz has been a considerable success. It has also had a lasting influence on Israeli society, its politics, culture and defence. But in order to survive it has had to modify its attitude to home life and the rearing of children. The founding fathers, in their socialist zeal and secularist conviction, overlooked the fact that the Chasidim went to their Rabbi from their homes, and that it was to their homes that they returned. They lived within the pull of both the master and the family. The future of the kibbutz depends on the restoration of that kind of tension, in which the best of the collective and the private can be allowed to merge. Similarly, the future of the bourgeois home will depend on the interaction between the community and the private sanctuary.

The difficult side of home and family need not be overlooked. Monogamy easily becomes synonymous with monotony, and the security of the home can well appear as a prison to its inhabitants. It is essential to be in touch with this 'shadowy' side of home life and try to diminish the burden it imposes. The interchange between home and community may very well serve as the framework within which the tension can be maintained and both home and Synagogue enriched. Within that tension security is possible. It goes beyond the quest of survival in that it addresses itself to the need of the individual and not only to the demand of the collective. By pointing to the intrinsic merits of the home, the Jewish dimension of that home becomes apparent and the Synagogue as a model is accessible.

Survival of the people through the security of the individual points to the future. The Sabbath can only be truly celebrated in the home. It is there that the serenity of the Messianic future comes within reach. The home is thus not only a realm of *being* that stands as a corrective to the world of *having*, but also a way of *becoming*, a laboratory for the better tomorrow, a pointer to the ideal existence which, in the perception of the Prophets, can be realized in time and space.

It is this dimension of growth and development, *becoming*, that justifies our discussion of the Jewish home in a chapter devoted to Jewish education. For it is here that real learning takes place. Primary education in Jewish tradition has always been the responsibility of the home; the community was to provide higher education. A father is referred to as *avi mori*, 'my father my teacher', and a mother as *immi morati*, 'my mother my teacher'. To be just a biological parent is not enough; such a parent only brings a man into this world, but a teacher brings him also into the world to come. The home that is both a sanctuary and a school points beyond itself and helps its inhabitants to grow and come nearer to God.

The Jewish home is, inevitably, a bourgeois home in which culture, Jewish and non-Jewish, is being promoted and created. Maybaum uses for 'culture' the Hebrew word *avodah*, the term used in this chapter to describe work and worship as study. For him, 'Jewish culture is the gift of the diaspora in which the Jew receives from the creative Christian the possibility of becoming creative himself'. It is a reminder 'of the mutual penetration of Judaism and Christianity and of the great harvest this mutual influence of the monotheistic religions has provided and will provide in the future'.[5] In virtually all his books, Maybaum stresses the bourgeois nature of Jewish existence and its bonds with and differences from Christianity and Islam. The future of that existence cannot, therefore, be a matter of indifference to our non-Jewish neighbours.

[5] ibid., p. 96.

21

Doing Torah

The Prophetic and the Priestly co-exist in Jewish tradition. The former is more likely to come to the fore in Torah as *learning*, when the will of God and the faith of Israel find their theoretical expression. The latter is reflected in Torah as *doing*, when God's commandments and the accumulated wisdom of His people find their practical application. Both the Synagogue and the home are institutions that ideally seek to give equal emphasis to both learning and doing. In real life the dual stress is difficult to maintain and, therefore, none of the three movements in Judaism has really succeeded in remaining authentic by applying Torah both as the voice of Prophets and the rules of Priests. Broadly speaking, Reform has been too Prophetic, preaching lofty ideas but offering few opportunities for 'a Jewish atmosphere', be it in the Synagogue or in the home. Orthodoxy, by contrast, has been too Priestly, so pre-occupied with the minutiae of observance that it has concealed the higher purpose behind it. Zionism, finally, has, in a sense, abandoned both Synagogue and home in favour of the State, thus seeking to replace the individual's involvement by the collective's dictates.

But Jewish tradition does not really permit us to choose one side in favour of the other; this is why it is best characterized through tension. Even if it seems reasonable to assert that Jewish survival depends solely on the restatement of Prophetic ideals, or on painstaking application of rules and laws, or of abandoning the old structures in favour of a collective which can protect the Jew from extinction, on closer examination it becomes apparent that none of these general panaceas really works. Therefore, when reflecting on the future of Judaism, we must try again and again to re-establish structures in which the dialectical relationship is allowed to exist and where glib simple solutions are avoided. There can thus be no question of suggesting that the future of Judaism depends on more education *or* on more practice, but it may depend on a proper relationship and balance between the two.

Since much of this chapter has been devoted to theory and to education, let us now discuss practice and observance as reflected in Jewish law. Modernist exponents of Judaism have often been reluctant to stress the importance of law, because, in laudable apologetic fashion, they have sought to react against the tendentious Christian description of Judaism as law – superseded, of course, by the Christian religion of love. Even educated Christians seem to be astonished that the commandment 'Love your neighbour as yourself' does not have its origin with Jesus and the New Testament but with Moses and the Hebrew Bible (*Leviticus* 19:18). Characteristically, this sentence is found amidst a set of laws, often paraphrasing the Ten Commandments, in which lofty ideas and practical observances are listed side by side as a hint that to separate between them is to falsify Judaism.

Those who prefer Christianity in its secularized form tend to retain the dictum about loving one's neighbour, but they do not quote it in full. For the sentence actually reads: 'Love your neighbour as yourself: *I am the Lord.*' It is the existence of God that necessitates our love of man. By loving our neighbour we do the will of God. By cutting God out of the modern script, we also invalidate the force of the commandment and reduce it to a general norm. In the same way as Christian societies have not been able to practise the commandment because Christian teaching has ignored its practical–legalistic setting, so atheistic–'humanist' societies have failed because they have ignored its theistic religious root. A society that seeks to safeguard the future – be it a State, a Synagogue or a home – must take both the 'practical' and the 'religious' basis into account.

To do that sentence full justice it is perhaps not enough even to quote it in full; the whole verse has to be considered: 'You shall not take vengeance or bear a grudge against your kinsfolk. *Love your neighbour as yourself: I am the Lord.*' The starting point of the universal commandment about love is a particularist setting referring to kinsfolk only. We have to begin with what is obvious and natural before we proceed to the general. That is why Jewish tradition has always assumed that before we can save the world, we must try to save ourselves and before we Jews can address ourselves to the problems of the world, we must try to put our own house in order. By starting with ourselves and trying to put our Jewish home in order, we are actually making a contribution to the welfare of society. And if others would emulate us and start with themselves, the process would be speeded up and salvation would be within reach. Once again the lofty universalistic – Prophetic – and the 'down-to-earth' practical – Priestly – interplay.

The words that follow immediately on the commandment to love our neighbour read: 'You shall observe My laws' (*Leviticus* 19:19). Even the commandment to love has to be translated into practical laws if it is to have any meaning. The general principle has to find its particular application. That is obviously true in the case of loving one's neighbour, but it is not different in the case of loving God. Law is legitimate not only when ethical principles have to be translated into tangible rules but also when religious precepts are to find their practical expression. Franz Rosenzweig called rituals 'gestures of love' and these are as much part of the celebrated *Leviticus* chapter and the Ten Commandments as are lofty moral norms.

How is that experience to be transmitted to future generations? The formula of Rabbinic Judaism depended on the dogma that Moses received both the written Torah (the Pentateuch) and the Oral Torah, i.e. the whole body of interpretation, from God and, therefore, both are immutable. Principles and precepts, ideas and observances all come from the same divine source and it is not for us to establish a hierarchy of importance but to try and do them all. Since the body of law is seen as an integral part of Torah, not imposed on it, dogmatic tradition expects the Jew to observe the whole body of rules as laid down by it. It is recognized that that may not be possible in practice for every individual at all times, but to do the maximum must remain his ideal. He may even escape the law, as long as he does not seek to challenge or alter it.

The fundamentalist view, however, is difficult to maintain consistently and even those who are prepared to follow Jewish tradition almost to the maximum, are not able to sustain it. Dogmatic Orthodoxy belongs to the Jewish Middle Ages, which vanished when the walls of the ghetto were finally broken down, and which can only be retained today in artificial enclaves where Orthodox extremists live. The Jew of today and, even more the Jew of tomorrow, will need a different vision, a vision that does not negate tradition but, at the same time, does affirm the findings of scholarship and common sense.

In his book, *We Have Reason to Believe*, which created a stir in Anglo–Jewish mainstream Orthodoxy when it appeared in 1957, Louis Jacobs laid the foundations of such a vision when, basing himself on sound scholarship, he wrote that 'many Jewish teachers conceived of revelation in more dynamic terms than the doctrine of "verbal" inspiration would imply. For them, revelation is an encounter between the divine and the human, so that there is a human as well as a divine factor in revelation, God revealing His Will not alone *to* men but *through* men.' [1] Jacobs follows the view expressed by other Jewish scholars that 'the Rabbis had a sound polemical motive in emphasizing that the whole of the Torah was given "at once" to Moses. They were chiefly concerned with a rebuttal of the Christian view that the Torah was a temporary institution, that there had been a "progressive revelation" and that, therefore, the "New Testament" could be looked upon as a culmination of the "Old".' [2]

Although what Jacobs had to tell the world was not particularly new to non-fundamentalist Jews and Christians, it is important to us, firstly, because it places the Jewish Liberal view of 'progressive revelation' where it belongs: as an imitation of Christian teaching, arrogantly assuming that *we* now know more than *they* did then, by the mere fact that we are moderns. Secondly, Jacobs' stance is important because he implies that a non-fundamentalist view is wholly consistent with Jewish tradition, despite the new scientific insights not available to the ancients: 'No doubt our new attitude to the Biblical record, in which, as the result of historical, literary and archaeological investigations, the Bible is seen against the

---

[1] Louis Jacobs, *We Have Reason to Believe* (Vallentine Mitchell 1957), p. 81.
[2] ibid., p. 76.

background of the times in which its various books were written, ascribes more to the human element than the ancients would have done, but this is a difference in degree, not in kind.'[3] Modernism is thus not a break with the past but a response to tradition in the light of present knowledge.

However, it is not only a matter of scientific evidence, but also a question of interpretation and application. Having accepted Torah as both theory and practice, and as both tradition and change, can we now make the purpose of Judaism fully evident?

Mordecai M. Kaplan defines a value as 'any attitude or belief which is stressed as of high worth, because of its importance for the impetus which it supplies to the striving for salvation'. For him 'the alternative to authoritative dogma which has to be accepted, regardless of reason's approval, is not credal anarchy. It is rather the acceptance of values which, without offending reason, are capable of satisfying our most distinctively human needs.'[4] Although he might not have approved of it himself, this definition seems to fit into our concept of *mitsvah*, the practical manifestation of Jewish law. Not only values but actions reflect the impetus to 'the striving for salvation' and are alternatives to both dogma and anarchy. For if the former represents totalitarian Orthodoxy, the latter reflects antinomian Reform; the future of Judaism cannot be based on either, but on democracy.

One of Kaplan's disciples and collaborators, Ira Eisenstein, has shown how democracy can be applied to Jewish observance.[5] Speaking of the present rather than the future, Eisenstein asserts, 'While our ancestors gladly accepted the yoke of the Torah, Jews today would prefer to have a hand in the fashioning of that yoke'. He reflects that 'when a person has a share in the making of a law, he has a stake in it, and is more likely to defend it from abuse or neglect'. Since Judaism is primarily a group religion, and 'all group life, Jewish included, must be governed by law if it is to retain any sem-

[3] ibid., p. 81.

[4] Mordecai M. Kaplan, *Basic Values in Jewish Religion* (Reconstructionist, New York, 1957), p. 3.

[5] Ira Eisenstein, 'The Need for Legislation in Jewish Law' in *Tradition and Change: The Development of Conservative Judaism*, edited by Mordecai Waxman (Burning Bush, New York, 1958), pp. 447–54.

blance of continuity with the past and unity in the present', the democratic principle should be applied. This would mean that rabbis would act as 'experts', the way lawyers advise a legislature or professional clerks a lay magistrate's court, but it is the people who must decide what they are going to observe and how they are to do it. The democratically agreed practice of a community will then also act as a model for the individual practice of its members. The congregation, based around a synagogue, will become the forum in which such decisions are made, now no longer along conventional denominational lines (Orthodox, Conservative, Reform, etc.) but reflecting the true needs and aspirations of its members. Only in this way can Jewish tradition – as taught and expounded by the rabbi, who now becomes a true teacher, not a priest who lives Judaism on behalf of his indifferent congregation – be blended with the needs of living Jews into a system which is neither dogmatic nor anarchic.

There are flaws in the democratic system. For example, it is not realistic to assume that the majority of any congregation, or even a sizeable proportion of its members, will wish to get involved in detailed discussions concerning observance. Decisions are bound to be made by a small clique, at best a 'cognitive minority'. Nevertheless, even such adverse circumstances provide the Jewish community with an opportunity to be educated and involved in a way that is precluded in the present denominational system. Moreover, the fact that the rabbi is to be cast in the role of 'resource person' and not vicarious Jew, is bound to change the climate of Jewish life. Finally, a democratic system would break down the hierarchic structure current in Israel, as well as in Orthodoxy in Britain and elsewhere, which provides for a 'chief' rabbi (or two, as in Israel) who is constitutionally entitled to direct his underlings.

Another objection to the democratic system is that it threatens the unity of the Jewish world by virtually allowing every congregation to make its own decisions. The implication of this charge is that unity prevails now, which, of course, is not the case. Not only are there sharp dividing lines between the various denominations, but even within each movement there are considerable differences. Thus Conservative congregations in California seem to be different from their counterparts on the East Coast of the United States, despite the fact that they belong to the same organization. The Canadian constituents of the Union of American Hebrew Congregations have a different outlook on basic issues affecting Jewish law to their colleagues in the United States. There are great differences between Reform Judaism in Europe, Israel and America. The divisions and diversities within Orthodoxy are legion. Jewish unity is a myth; there is little to suggest that Jewry will be less united where democracy prevails in individual communities, not only in matters of election of officers but also in questions of how to observe Judaism. On the contrary, there is much to suggest that 'the will of the people' is more uniform than the needs of organizational leaders who manipulate the people.

These leaders, including rabbis, often have vested interests in holding cynical views about the ignorance and incompetence of the masses in order to enhance their own importance and authority. They tend to overlook the genuine search for a religious lifestyle in which many modern laymen and laywomen would like to engage. The fact that these lay people remain uninvolved has more to do with lack of opportunities than with lack of interest. By exposing ordinary Jews to decisions about seemingly minor practical matters and pointing to the grounds for and implications of these decisions, something of the latent enthusiasm can be kindled. Once again the combination of theoretical learning and practical action can reflect the Torah in its full glory.

Although this may seem a radical departure from what is currently happening in the Jewish world, where authoritarianism and apathy feed upon each other, there is precedence for allowing the people to shape Jewish observance. Herbert Loewe points to it in his Introduction to *A Rabbinic Anthology* which he edited jointly with Claude Montefiore: 'It is an adage in Judaism that potent though the *Din* (Law) may be, though it "cleave the mountain", yet custom (*Minhag*) prevails over *Din*, for it is in the guidance of the people that Revelation operates: *vox populi* emphatically is *vox Dei*. Is there not a tremendous significance in this? Do we not here see the divine Revelation manifested in the evolution of history?' [6] He re-

---

[6] C. G. Montefiore and H. Loewe, *A Rabbinic Anthology* (JPSA, Philadelphia, 1960), p. xxvi.

cognizes that '*vox populi* might so easily be vox *diaboli*' but records that it never became that. It is possible that the efforts to put Jewish living on to a democratic footing may fail, but that need not happen. The experience of Judaism of past ages gives us courage to attempt such a radical reconstruction now. The alternative may be atrophy.

By stressing the need to integrate study with practice, *learning* Torah with *doing* Torah, and suggesting the democratic principle as a traditionally acceptable method, I am advocating a different kind of balance in Jewish observance between skills and experience. Conventionally, Orthodox Judaism has worked on the assumption that once a person acquires the knowledge *how* to do things, he will also appreciate the *why* of doing them. Reform Judaism reacted against this myth by pointing to all the men, who though well versed in the skills of Judaism nevertheless have rejected its aims. It therefore originally reversed the order and, in predictable rationalist fashion, believed that it could teach purpose which would either lead to the acquisition of skills or, more likely, result in the removal of the need for skills. When the fashion in the world of religion shifted from rationalism to mysticism, the stress on rationale was replaced by an interest in experience. The same shift was also perceived in Orthodox circles; the remarkable success of neo-Chasidism, e.g. in the manifestation of the Lubavitch movement, is a product of it. But experience without structure, even at its best, leads to syncretism and, as a result, both Reform and Orthodox 'revivalism' began to look like something else.

When we recognize the importance of experience, not through artificial effects of silent meditation at the lakeside, or 'the third Sabbath meal' in dimly lit rooms, but through the blend of doing and learning which also involves the will of the people, we are helping to create a new kind of balance of forces in Jewish life. In stressing the collective aspect of our endeavour we accept the fact that such experience is more easily attained in the community than in the home. In the same way as the temporary spread of idolatry made the Book of *Deuteronomy* stress centralized worship in preference to private shrines, so the temporary breakdown of home and family forces us to stress the community in preference to the home, and community worship will assume greater significance. Before the home can regain its true significance, we need to provide a framework for religious experience within a traditional setting. The Synagogue as presently constituted is well equipped to offer it: it often has access to a rabbi; it is run by a 'cognitive minority' of committed Jews; by its very architecture it places Torah in the centre; it serves as a model for Jewish life. True, it has become the victim of secularization, but it need not remain so. It is possible to restore it as a House of God *through which*, not *instead of which*, the real needs of the people are met.

One of the reasons for the validity of Judaism put forward in the Preface is that it gives access to a unique source of wisdom, Torah in the widest sense of the word. There is a vast and rich literature, both ancient and modern, in most of the world's major languages, that seeks to articulate and expound such wisdom. But for the contemporary Jew to benefit from the teaching, and perhaps also share it with his non-Jewish neighbour, a new method of study and practice is required. The aim of this chapter has been not to restate the content of the wisdom but to point to a new approach to it in the belief that it is on the latter that our future depends. Only by adopting a new methodology can the old teachings meet the needs of the contemporary Jew and thus motivate him to commit himself to work for a future for Judaism, beyond his vague desire to see it survive in the present. As the Jewish world is currently constituted, none of the existing branches have, so far, been able to evolve a consistent way of making the ancient heritage of Torah our possession today, although each have made advances and gained new insights. To secure the future we must endeavour to integrate what is best in each into a more unified pattern and thus go beyond current denominational boundaries.

VI

THE FUTURE OF ISRAEL

Out of the Ghetto and into the World

I don't see how one can think about
being a Jew today without the notion of
Exile. That is certainly true also for
anybody who cares about trying to be
a Jew in America. For us, Exile specifically means being willing to take upon
oneself the burdens of being an individual in relationship to one's faith and
fighting for the welfare of the Jewish
people most of whose members are
largely indifferent and don't care.

Eugene B. Borowitz[1]

[1] *Sh'ma – a Journal of Jewish Responsibility*, 10/185, 11 January 1979.

22

The Jew and the State

Encounter with God is difficult and painful; Jacob was maimed at Peniel. Therefore, Jews both in the past and today, have sought and found substitutes. I have suggested that the Torah has served as such a substitute. When Jews became part of the Western world and Torah was secularized into 'education' and 'culture', the mystical relationship between Torah and Israel, which at times simulated the relationship between God and Israel, was weakened or abandoned: Torah ceased to be a bride and became a quaint museum piece; the love-letter turned into a dead-letter; the marriage contract may not have been cancelled but it was definitely rendered inoperative. The emancipated Jew was shedding both God and Torah from his Jewishness.

However, the weakened mystical relationship between Israel, the 'groom', and Torah, the 'bride', was replaced by some people with another mystical relationship, promised by Zionism and, in a sense, consummated by the establishment of the State of Israel: the relationship between the masculine People of Israel and the feminine Land of Israel came to take the place of the relationship between Israel and Torah, which in turn had once replaced the bond in 'marriage' between Israel and God. In some minds the feminine *erets* (land) and the equally feminine *medina* (state) were confused and interchanged: the bond to the Land became to many identical with the bond to the State. There is much in current Israeli life, and in the attitude of the Jewish Diaspora to the Jewish State, which can best be understood in terms of this secular neo-mysticism. The sense of strength and potency that settlers felt once they had come to live on the land in Israel was a manifestation of an almost mystical union between People and Land. The Diaspora's dependence on the Jewish State and

the feeling that only Israel possesses the necessary strength
for Jewish continuity and survival was another expression of
the phenomenon. The loss of confidence on the part of many
Israelis and the growing determination by many Diaspora
Jews to speak out independently and critically in the last few
years, after the 1973 Yom Kippur War, is therefore a sign of
a serious crisis, for it implies a threat to dissolve a bond that
was once considered sacred. But it is also the promise of a
radical re-evaluation of the role of the Jewish people and its
real dependence on God. The disillusionment with the State
may bring us back to Torah and to God. By recognizing the
'feminine', dependent, element in us as a People we may be
able to rediscover something of our true identity, based on
our bonds with not only the Land but also with God and
Torah.

The Rabbis could keep the pagan dimension of their glorification of the Torah in check by regarding it as having been
given by God. For Torah to be our possession, God was
necessary. Jews who today still treat the Holy Land in the
way in which their ancestors once treated Holy Writ also try
to see it as God-given and therefore regard its borders as
sacred as every letter of the Torah. But the idolatrous element
in their fervour is unmistakable. We have often been quick
to point out idolatry in Christianity where the belief in God's
only-begotten Son makes God necessary though not quite
operational, but have not been prepared to see the same tendencies both in Jewish religious fundamentalism and in Jewish
'religious' nationalism, which identifies Jewish spirituality
with settlement on the land that God promised the Patriarchs.
Although we must beware of drawing too many parallels between other nationalist movements, many of which have made
us Jews their victims, and our own, we cannot afford to be
blind to the similarities as far as ill effects are concerned.

It would be an oversimplification to say that the Jews first
abandoned God in favour of Torah and then both for the sake
of the Land and the State, but the tendency is there. The
indivisible unity between God, Torah and Israel has been split
up, each movement in Judaism stressing one at the expense
of the others: Reform became the spokesman of God, Orthodoxy of Torah and Zionism of Israel. In the same way as I
have tried to suggest how we must affirm God, free from

denominational interests, and to interpret Torah in an old/
new way, let me now propose ways of affirming Israel so that
it neither negates the Land nor spurns the State and, at the
same time, affirms the Diaspora and seeks to embrace the
world.

To start with, we must look at our basic attitude to the
State, any State. Ignaz Maybaum has written:

> When I sing 'God Save the Queen' I do it both with hap-
> piness and with sincerity. I am a Jew of many countries.
> My English passport is the fourth I hold. My first one was
> an Hungarian, my second an Austrian, my third a German.
> I am a Jew driven out from Germany where I spent the
> formative years of my life and where I settled down and
> where I thought I would live all my life. I became a refugee,
> driven out from the country which I had learned to love.
> All this explains my happiness and sincerity when singing:
> God Save the Queen, and I feel I am obeying the solemn
> commandment of Jeremiah who wrote to the Jewish people
> in Babylon: 'And seek the peace of the city whither I have
> caused you to be carried away captives, and pray unto the
> Lord for it: for in the peace thereof shall ye have peace.'
> (29:7)[1]

According to Maybaum the Jew's loyalty to the State in
which he lives is based on a mixture of intrinsic merits of the
regime that prevails there and obedience to the Biblical command. Jews have always been prepared to be loyal citizens,
working far beyond the line of duty, and irrespective of actual
rewards, when they were allowed to do so in freedom and
dignity. The enthusiasm and skill that many of them displayed
once a Jewish State was proclaimed stemmed from a basic
predisposition frustrated by cruel circumstances in the Diaspora, but now able to express itself. Precisely because we have
not been able to take the State for granted but have had to
judge it on its merits, living in exile for most of our history,
and out of our resolve to obey God's word, we have been able
to relate to it in a way different from other peoples.

However, no amount of enthusiasm and loyalty justifies
blind obedience to the State, for that would mean replacing

[1] Ignaz Maybaum, *The Faith of the Jewish Diaspora* (Vision 1962), p. 145f.

the eternal with the temporal, which is idolatry. By elevating the State to something super-human, the ideal is identified with the expedient, the Messianic future is confused with the less than perfect present. Idols cannot exist in the realm of God, and the State is a potential idol. In the words of Erich Fromm, 'God, as the supreme value and goal, is *not* man, the state, an institution, nature, power, possession, sexual powers, or any artifact made by man'. Fromm asserts that 'the history of mankind up to the present time is primarily the history of idol worship, from the primitive idols of clay and wood to the modern idols of the state, the leader, production and consumption'.[2] To be himself and to realize his purpose, the Jew has to keep away from that history and to pursue his own goal. That is his Prophetic task, which Fromm calls humanism. To achieve it he must deploy Priestly methods but, when the latter masks the former, decline, even decay, sets in.

The fact that Maybaum, and so many Jews with him, both in earlier epochs and in our days, have had a succession of passports is, according to Fromm (also a refugee from Nazi Germany) a blessing in disguise: 'What from a mundane standpoint was the tragedy of the Jews – the loss of their country and their state – from the humanist standpoint was their greatest blessing: being among the suffering and despised, they were able to develop and uphold a tradition of humanism.'[3] Being forced by circumstances, however cruel, to remain 'rootless' and 'cosmopolitan' has given Jews a particular perspective which makes us refuse to compromise with the vision for the sake of political conformity. No wonder, then, that the totalitarian regime in Russia uses the term 'rootless cosmopolitan' as a word of abuse, frequently especially directed against the Jew.

For despite all the loyalty and devotion, the State in which I live and of which I am a citizen can only be viewed as a temporary abode. This is not only due to the fact that Jews always recall persecutions and expulsions from countries that once were friendly and welcoming, but also because Judaism sets its sights on the ideal future, the Messianic kingdom, and

[2] Erich Fromm, *You Shall be as Gods* (Jonathan Cape 1967), p. 43.
[3] ibid., p. 15.

everything that appears to be replacing it, or imitating it, must be regarded as an idol. Therefore a perspective on the future must ultimately be critical of the State even when, for the sake of survival, certain States are affirmed and where loyalty and enthusiasm is a legitimate expression both of self-interest and of religious obligation.

This in no way curbs the Jews' capacity to give of their best to the State. On the contrary, it is precisely because we accept ourselves as living *in* the State without being *of* it that we are keen to justify our existence by contributing to its welfare, for our existence depends on its stability and success. Since we do not feel that we really belong, we have a duty to justify our existence on merit. As we do not take anything for granted, we make sure that we give at least as much as we receive.

Historically, the giving and the receiving was done primarily in the private domain. The State is necessary, and laudable when liberal, but it is transient. Maybaum places the State in juxtaposition to the family and insists that it is the latter more than the former that creates the conditions for a Messianic future. That is why some of the contribution that the Jew makes as a citizen is in his capacity as a member of a law-abiding, industrious family, which discharges its civic responsibilities and, in addition, supports causes that promote social equality and cultural openness. As a result, Jews have tended to be more prominent in academic and cultural life, in commercial, professional and social activities than in the public arena of politics. For the Jew who seeks prominence in political life almost invariably has to abandon his Jewish commitment for the sake of his career.

The withdrawal into the relatively private domain, away from the precarious arena of politics, is inherent in the Jewish stress on family life. But it has also at least two other reasons: the nature of the State itself and anti-Semitism.

Even the democracies in which we live force us into ever greater collectivism and bureaucracy. That is inherent in the burden of running a complex modern State and there is very little that we can do about it. Any alternative political system is unlikely to be better. When a religious tradition, such as Judaism, stresses family and community, it is bound to come into conflict with the power of the State. And when religionists believe that they can overcome the conflict by becoming themselves involved in the politics of the State, they soon discover that they have to compromise with their religious ideals. If they do not, they become irrelevant and quixotic. In either case, secularism – on which the modern State thrives – carries the day.

The State of Israel is a case in point. It started off with the highest ideals and it still cherishes them. But reality forces constant compromise. Without compromise the Jewish State could not survive to implement its lofty principles. Religionists who withdraw from statecraft and politics as being too 'impure' and too incompatible with what they stand for, leave the arena to the secularists for whom expediency is the highest goal. In this way the noble aims of Judaism get ignored. Religious people who organize themselves into political parties, as has happened, for example, with Israel's Orthodoxy, soon find out that they can only stay in the game if they compromise with what they stand for and 'secularize' their religious stance. Much of the *malaise* of Israeli life is caused by this vicious circle.

Once again, therefore, neither negation of the political system nor collusion with it is required, but tension: not *either* the State *or* religion, but *both* the State *and* religion. The ancient Prophets expressed it in their attitude to the King. In the same way as they acted as correctives to the ritualism of Priests so they saw it as their task to act as correctives to the politicizing of Kings. In the same way as they pointed to religious values beyond the minutiae of observance, so they pointed to social values beyond the compromise of politics. The Prophets rejected neither the Temple nor the State but they criticized both in order to improve them. They left us with a legacy and a formula. Eugene Borowitz has described it as 'creative social maladjustment'.[4] It is the most coherent formula for religious life in relation to the State. Once again it points to encounter, not confrontation; dialogue, not rejection. It is the condition of Exile, even when Jews live in their own country.

Undoubtedly, this attitude will offer new ammunition to

[4] Eugene B. Borowitz, *Facing Up To It* (Reform Synagogues of Great Britain 1967), p. 35.

the anti-Semites. But by now Jews should have realized that anti-Semitism is primarily the problem of the Gentiles. There is nothing Jews can do to remove it. Even when they try to disappear from the face of the earth, anti-Semitism does not let them. If they participate in politics, they bring evidence of 'the Jewish world conspiracy'. If they withdraw into the family and community, they are in danger of being accused as 'parasites'. On the whole, Jews have preferred the latter to the former risks and stayed out of political life. It is changing to some extent at the moment, but that does not mean that the new order will prevail. Even those assimilated Jews who now see themselves as equals and entitled to participate in the affairs of the State may have to face the truth the way Jewish politicians – or, to be more precise, politicians of Jewish origin – had to face it in the Weimar Republic and in Soviet Russia: as soon as the going gets rough, they are the most obvious scapegoats.

23

The Jew and the State of Israel

What is true of the relationship of the Jew to the State in general must also, to a large extent, be true of the attitude of the Jew to the State of Israel. The passage by Ignaz Maybaum quoted earlier, expressing the author's happiness when singing the British national anthem, continues in this way:

> When I sing the Hatikvah, the Jewish national anthem, I think of my brethren in Israel. I pray for them with sincerity. I must stress this sincerity because I hold no brief for the ideology which demands that every Jew should settle in Israel. The sincerity of my prayer for Israel is mixed with anxiety about the dangerous political situation in which my brethren in Israel have to live.[1]

A dichotomy between the country in which I live and my commitment to Israel, or a conflict of loyalties, is not really called for. Jewish existence is a tension between dispersion and homeland, expressed by my ability to sing the national anthems of both countries with sincerity. By accepting myself as an heir of a tradition that regards every State only as an interim solution, I can accept several such solutions simultaneously because none is complete and thus exclusive of others. The real goal is the Kingdom of God. Earthly kingdoms are stations on the way, and those who rule there are subject to God's law, of which we are the custodians. Some such stations are good and beneficial, so we affirm them; others are harmful and dangerous and we must oppose them. The religious perspective enables us to be cosmopolitan and

---

[1] Maybaum, op. cit., p. 146. I have changed the idiosyncratic *hatiquah* in the passage to Hatikvah, as it is normally spelled and recognized by most readers and writers.

internationalist without in any way being indifferent or uncommitted.

When the religious dimension is weakened or lost, idolatry takes its place and, as Fromm puts it, the modern State is one manifestation of such idolatry. Emancipated Jews who had abandoned their religious tradition wanted to express their secularism in the same way as their non-Jewish neighbours, which included politics and the veneration of the State. When anti-Semitism severely hampered them in their endeavours, or prevented them from participating altogether, they sought other ways of expressing themselves. One such way was to elevate the notion of a Jewish State to the status of their perception of the State in which they lived. The intransingence and prejudice of non-Jews have as much to do with the emergence of Zionism as has the love of Zion as embodied in Jewish literature and liturgy. Many early Zionists argued that if the Gentiles would not allow us to be equal citizens in the countries where we were born, we must endeavour to become such citizens in the land in which our people originated and towards which our ancestors have looked. The State of Israel is a glorious fusion of the noble aspirations of the Jewish people and the murderous devices of their enemies: one of the many miracles in Jewish history.

However, as long as the country in which I live enables me to live in peace and in dignity, it deserves my loyalty. That loyalty need in no way be challenged or diminished by my commitment to and deep concern for my fellow Jews everywhere, not least in the Jewish State. I know the price they had to pay to have a country of their own and I fear that, if their existence there is threatened, a fate even worse than the gas chambers awaits them. Maybaum's prayer for Israel, mixed with anxiety for her inhabitants, expresses an important aspect of the reality of contemporary Judaism.

Some Israelis say that the only way to lessen the anxiety is for Jews to go and live in Israel. There is, however, little evidence that that is so and much to suggest that Israel's future is as much bound up with a strong Diaspora as it is with a dominant Jewish element in her own population. But even if Israel's security would increase because of increased immigration of Jews, the concentration of Jews in one country and the identification of Judaism with one State would mean the end of Judaism as we have known it since the days of the Prophets. And that is a price that even the threat to the State of Israel must not compel us to pay.

The question as to whether all Jews should go and live in Israel or not illustrates well the issue of survival *versus* purpose. The stress on survival as the ultimate aim of Jewish existence is the product of secularization and as such is inimical to Judaism. The insistence that purpose takes precedence because it implies survival, but goes beyond it, reflects the religious mood.

And yet, when all is said and done, it is impossible to be a Jew without relating to the State of Israel in a particular way. Without wishing to claim mystical powers of the land, or a component in the air of Israel which makes for Prophecy – such claims and many others have been made over the ages and are still being made – we cannot ignore the fact that virtually no Jew can encounter Israel the way he encounters other countries.

Elsewhere[2] I have described the State of Israel as a metaphor for hope. Without its establishment in 1948 it is doubtful whether the surviving Jews would have seen much point in continuing as Jews. Without its existence and influence over Jewish life everywhere it is doubtful whether the Jews in the Western Diaspora, notably in the United States, would have had the resources to train a new generation in Judaism, and it is known that the Jews in Russia would have had no opportunity to rediscover their origins and their purpose. Without the Israeli victory in 1967, it is questionable whether Judaism could have remained credible to the Jews.

Eugene Borowitz wrote shortly after the Six Day War that 'in one incredible week we reclaimed two strands of our old Jewish hope: we saw God save our people Israel; and we recognized personally how our individual being was tied to our Covenant folk. And now we could feel free to speak of what had sounded so hollow in the post-Holocaust days, that we, personally and individually, have from time to time felt His helping presence in our lives.' As a result of the experiences of Israel and her deliverance, the Messianic perspective

[2] 'Towards a Zionist Ideology for Reform Judaism' in Dow Marmur (editor), *A Genuine Search* (Reform Synagogues of Great Britain 1979), pp. 200–8.

of Judaism rang true again: 'Gladly would we await the Messiah with the normal tests of endurance. Yet in the midst of whatever bondage history may now bring, we can once again hope in His action on our behalf. He did so for our fathers. He did so in our time. We trust He will do so again for our children and our children's children. His Covenant with us remains unbroken.' [3]

Zionism today is, or should be, the reiteration of that hope and the determination to do all that needs doing in order to merit that unbroken Covenant and to remain a full partner to it. The State of Israel gives us Jews an opportunity to express our commitment to our heritage relatively undisturbed by others. It is thus not only a question of living a life 'like all the nations', but, above all, living like Jews. Because Israel, the people, is bound to both God and to Torah, the State of Israel cannot free itself from similar bonds. Its existence is conditioned by the two other components and the two others are affected by the destiny of the people of Israel in its land and everywhere else.

The fact that Israel is the metaphor for hope does not mean, however, that the Messianic era is already at hand. The existence of the Jewish State makes it possible for us to wait patiently for the ideal future and to make the best of exilic existence. More than a decade after his analysis of Jewish hope in the light of the victory at the Six Day War, Borowitz summarized a symposium on 'what we learned from the 1970s' in this way.

So no one here seems to think in terms of what the normal American Jew would understand, that the State of Israel *per se*, without this theological context, has absolute value for Jews. I repeat, it is most unusual that no one in this room seems ready to defend what is normally taken as the central effective reality of Jewish life. Perhaps then, we may conclude that at least as far as certain thoughtful, sensitive, committed American Jews are involved, the time of the Israelo-centrism of American Jewish life has passed.

The second thing that I hear of some importance is that, anybody who cares seriously about being a Jew is in Exile

[3] Eugene B. Borowitz, 'Hope Jewish and Hope Secular', in *Judaism*, xvii, 2 (Spring 1968), p. 146.

and would be in Exile even if that person were in Jerusalem. That Exile results because our Jewish ideal is unrealised anywhere in the world. Indeed Exile might be even worse for a Jew in the State of Israel because one expects more of it and of Jews as masters of their own household than of Jews elsewhere.[4]

The State of Israel has Messianic potential and that potential is fulfilled only to the extent that 'our Jewish ideal' is being realized. That ideal, whatever else it is, must include social justice in general and, more specifically, love of the stranger, 'for you were strangers in the land of Egypt' (*Leviticus* 19:34). The basis of both justice and love is the concluding phrase of that verse: 'I the Lord am your God'. Our critique of the State of Israel and its policies is based on this perspective; it is the Prophetic censure of the King.

The Prophet, we have said, to be credible must be an insider. Does not that mean that only Israelis are fit to criticize Israel? That question has to be answered in the affirmative. That is why it is not for me here to express views on Israeli policies, but merely to seek to explain the relationship between Israel and the Diaspora in the overall context of Jewish purpose. Our attitude to Israel cannot be determined by the economic or political conditions that prevail at any given period. It must be viewed in the context of the tension between the three components of Jewish existence and by realizing that that tension cannot be constrained within a State, however crucial that State may be for the affirmation that the Covenant between God and His people has not been broken.

The State of Israel implies both danger and opportunity. An Israeli political scientist, Dan V. Segre, writes:

> On the one hand, the emergence of the Jewish State did not stop the process of assimilation by the Israeli Jew to alien cultures but only transferred this process from the level of the individual to the collective. The trend to create for the Jews 'a state like any other state' has been accompanied by the desire to create in Israel a society of Jews like any other society – which leads to serious identity problems, if Jews are to remain Jews. On the other hand, the very

[4] *Sh'ma* 10/85, 11 January 1979.

fact of the physical return of large numbers of Jews to their ancestral land . . . has in many ways brought the Israelis back to the sources of their own civilization.[5]

How to curb this collective assimilation whilst taking full advantage of the prospect of Jewish renewal is for Segre, and indeed for all concerned Jews, the great challenge: 'The central question of Zionism and Israel, the "new Jewish Question", is turning from the problem of physical survival to that of spiritual survival, and of the ability to resist the pressures of the new, pagan world.'[6] Segre too is thus pre-occupied with the shift from the quest for survival to the search for purpose.

The religious dimension of that shift is not lost on him, when he agonizes over 'the theopolitical question of the direction in which the secular Zionist state will develop: that of the traditional covenant or that of the materialistic modern world'.[7] He hopes for a political system which 'works on a triangular relationship: the people, the élite, and God who remains the essential link between the people and the élite'.[8]

In Segre's scheme of things the dichotomy between Israel and Diaspora is false, for although the physical conditions of Exile became intolerable, the spiritual structure as shaped by the self-same Exile became crucial to Jewish identity:

The Israelis were right to accept the Zionist theory that the abnormal Diaspora conditions of the Jews could be cured by their return as free men to their own land; but they were wrong in believing that a Jewish state could do away with the old Jewish values which had maintained the Jewish identity for millennia. These values were, in fact, the very source of that inner strength, self-assurance, and self-respect which had permitted and could still permit the Jewish nation to face the trying fate which history has imposed upon it.[9]

To normalize the abnormal situation without destroying the

[5] Dan V. Segre, *A Crisis of Identity – Israel and Zionism* (Oxford University Press 1980), p. 11.
[6] ibid., p. 17.
[7] ibid., p. 73.
[8] ibid., p. 78.
[9] ibid., p. 84.

value system now becomes central to the Jewish purpose, taking us far beyond the immediate objective of 'mere' survival. To achieve that objective both Israel and Diaspora are needed; they need each other and Judaism needs them both. Therefore, the choice is not between *either* Israel *or* the Diaspora and even less between nationalism and assimilation, as some secularists would have it. Jewish existence prompts us to acknowledge *both* the Jewish State *and* the world. The future of Judaism rests on this integrated view. Those who wish to create a dichotomy jeopardize that future, however much they may insist that they are truly concerned about Jewish survival. But we may be forced into such a false choice between the State of Israel and the People of Israel by anti-Semitism masquerading as anti-Zionism and wishing to annihilate the Jewish State in the name of some lofty principle, reflecting the hypocrisy of the non-Jewish world in a new guise. In the face of that Jews will have to close their ranks, despite all theological reservations, for even if the future of Judaism is not solely bound up with the State of Israel, it is inconceivable without it.

24

The Chosen People

Both the preceding chapters in this section, one about the attitude of the Jew to the State in general and the other about his relationship to the Jewish State, ended with reflections on anti-Semitism. For the Jew's reluctance to be identified completely with the State in which he lives can be easily used by his enemies as evidence of his disloyalty, even though the opposite is the truth, and his reservations about Israel can be taken by unscrupulous propagandists as a legitimization of their condemnation of the Jewish State. To avert this dual danger Jews have been prone to overstress their loyalty to the countries in which they live, even to the point of condoning evil, e.g. in South Africa, and at the same time they have suppressed even the mildest forms of criticism of Zionist ideology or Israeli policy. Once again, it seems, anti-Semitism is forcing us Jews to adopt attitudes which are alien and inimical to the teachings of Judaism. Since our future depends on these teachings being expressed and developed, it is necessary for us to free ourselves from the fetters imposed by anti-Semitism and take risks in our quest for survival in order to make it possible for our purpose to manifest itself.

The issues involved in such self-liberation are crystallized in our understanding of what it means to be 'the chosen people'. The Jewish doctrine of election has often been seen as a primary cause of anti-Semitism. We were told repeatedly that if we only could regard ourselves as having no special role, persecution would cease. However, not only is there no evidence that this would be the case, for anti-Semitism seems to flourish irrespective of what Jews do, and even in places where Jews have hardly ever been, but even if it were true, what would be the point of Jewish continuity and purpose without a specific role for Jews and Judaism? How long is it possible to survive merely in order to prevent Hitler from having another posthumous victory? Therefore, if we are to regard the existence of the Jewish people as necessary, we cannot escape the issue of chosenness. Traditional Orthodoxy has understood it primarily in terms of separation from the Gentiles and it thus has come to form the basis of much religious fanaticism and nationalist extremism. This, in a sense, was a reaction to the secularist–Zionist endeavour to make Jews like all other peoples, and the Jewish State like all other states, in the hope of thus eliminating anti-Semitism. Classical Reform has until recently stood outside Jewish nationalism precisely because it could only perceive of election as a 'mission to the Gentiles' contingent upon the ability of Jews to live among the nations as equal citizens with them, and it has shunned Orthodoxy for its exclusiveness.

The universalist–Reform view has been discredited with the advent of Hitler and the triumph of modern anti-Semitism. Events have shown that the Jew is not allowed to live as an equal citizen, however hard he may try. The secularist–Zionist view has been severely challenged by the very existence of the State of Israel, which can only justify itself as a specific Jewish State – and Jewish must mean in some way 'religious' – in sharp contrast to the clamour of the Palestine Liberation Organization for 'a secular democratic state'. Segre's analysis in this context is pertinent. Particularist Orthodoxy is currently endangering both Jewish teaching and the security of the Jewish State by claiming territories on the grounds that, according to Holy Writ, God has given them to His Chosen People. Once again the three streams in contemporary Judaism seem to be failing us. How, then, are we to look upon ourselves today in order to formulate our Judaism for tomorrow?

Jewish sources, from the Bible until modern times, have almost invariably spoken of a special relationship between God and His people. The Prophets and the Rabbis have viewed that relationship in marriage terms: the link between monogamy and monotheism has deep roots in Jewish consciousness. In this sense, then, God has chosen Israel to be 'His treasured possession', the wife that a husband takes for himself.

Since the Emancipation, however, the question of chosenness has been a cause of embarrassment to modernist Jews. Hence the secularist attempt to eliminate it and the non-Orthodox religious effort to reinterpret it. Even fundamentalist Orthodoxy, determined not to compromise with tradition, has kept quiet about chosenness until relatively recently, when it became a kind of argument in favour of settling in Judea and Samaria, territories once part of Erets Yisrael but now considered Arab. On the whole, Jews have been embarrassed by the notion of chosenness and have preferred to say as little as possible about it, especially when expounding their beliefs to non-Jews, for one could never be sure what anti-Semites would make of it.

In its secularized form the reticence included a denial that Jews may have certain propensities that are desirable and laudable. Thus the long tradition of stress on learning was played down in order not to evoke hostility. Presumably it is this desire that prompted Peter Gay to suggest that 'there is a historical and sociological study that desperately needs to be undertaken: that of stupid Jews'. He believes that 'the material would be abundant, and the results would correct the widespread and untenable notion that Jews are by endowment more intelligent than other people'.[1] One wonders whether that too is not an expression of Jewish embarrassment, for, surely, it is not likely to make any difference to anti-Semitic prejudice. But the doctrine of chosenness, even in its secularized and distorted form, evokes defence in Jews, particularly in 'marginal' Jews who by their alienation from their own people feel particularly exposed to anti-Semitism.

Gentiles have not liked the doctrine either. Christians have been taught to assume that the Church is the true heir of Israel and that the New Covenant had once and for all replaced the Old Covenant. Anti-Semites have seen in the doctrine conclusive evidence that the Jews believe themselves to have the right to rule the world and, therefore, are dangerous unless they are destroyed. The more others have adopted extremist views about their own chosenness, e.g. Christians or Nazis, the more have they projected it on the Jews and in so doing have legitimized their need to exterminate their ri-

[1] Peter Gay, *Freud, Jews and other Germans* (Oxford University Press 1979), p. 99.

vals. The impact of this has been so profound that even sympathetically inclined Gentiles have found the Jewish notion of a special relationship to God an embarrassment.

Since the basis of this doctrine is the affirmation of God and the acceptance of Revelation, of which the Torah is a document, a rejection of religion means that both secularized Jews and secularized Gentiles regard it as legitimate to refute the doctrine. Once that was done, it became possible to regard Jews like any other people. But by regarding Jews like any other people, I have suggested, the existence and future of Judaism becomes irrelevant and unimportant.

It is a view widely held by many secularized Jews and Gentiles who believe that the end of the Jewish people is now only a matter of time. Their voice has been so powerful that even religionists have been persuaded by it and the current clamour for survival is the outcome. I have tried to show that they speak with the voices of Satan. One way of substantiating that accusation is by pointing to a proper understanding of what chosenness really means.

The decision cannot be made on the basis of exegesis. Both the Bible and Rabbinic literature say so many things about what it means to be 'a peculiar people' that almost any view will find its support in the sources. We are, therefore, not really in a position to decide which is *the* authentic interpretation. Let us instead attempt to state what *ought to be* the Jewish view of election in the light of the challenge of the coming years and decades. The limitations of Orthodox extremism, Reform liberalism and Zionist rejection are obvious: the first, implying Jewish superiority, leads to fundamentalist exclusivity; the second, based on the notion of a mission to the Gentiles, is a manifestation of a sense of superiority no less objectionable than the one propounded by Orthodoxy; the third, insisting that Jews are no different from other nations, is unrealistic and untrue.

Chosenness, in the last resort, is an affirmation:

You have affirmed this day that the Lord is your God, that you will walk in His ways, that you will observe His laws and commandments and rules, and that you will obey Him. And the Lord has affirmed this day that you are, as He promised you, His treasured people which shall observe all

His commandments, and that He will set you, in fame and renown and glory, high above all the nations that He has made; and that you shall be, as He promised, a holy people to the Lord your God. (*Deuteronomy* 26:17–19).

The Covenant is expressed in words. The word we translate as 'affirmed' comes from the Hebrew root 'to say'. To be chosen means to choose by declaring one's allegiance. It does not begin with God who chooses us, but with us who choose God. The chosen are those who are prepared to take upon themselves the commandments as understood by tradition. It is written, 'You will observe His laws and commandments and rules'. It does not say: *all* of them! Not only those who observe everything are entitled to regard themselves as chosen, but all who declare their commitment to the Jewish way of life.

Chosenness is thus not a matter of divine initiative but of human endeavour. It is man's affirmation of God by doing His commands that evokes God's response and makes the individual a part of His people. Election is not based on birth but on commitment. It need not imply that every individual has to make it for himself; being part of a tradition implicates him in the endeavours of the collective, the foundation of which is religious rather than merely social and manifest in a lifestyle dedicated to God.

Anybody who wishes to make the affirmation, either by an act of conversion or 'merely' by identifying with the community and the people into which he was born, belongs to God's 'treasured possession'.

An often quoted Rabbinic legend tells of how God originally disclosed Himself to all the nations of the world, but each wanted to know what the Torah contained before committing themselves. Whenever God offered a sample, they soon found reason to reject it and the rest with it. When He came to the Israelites, they said immediately, 'All that the Lord has spoken we will do' (*Exodus* 19:8), so He gave the Torah to them. It was, therefore, really Israel that chose God and in this way was chosen by Him. By continued reaffirmation of the Torah the Jew earns his right to be part of the Chosen People. The reward of that choice ultimately outweighs all risks, for as

Keith Ward, a Christian theologian, has shown this is the way
to true belief:

> A religion may be characterized as a social organized way
> of relating men to the sacred; and a person becomes a
> religious believer when he commits himself to such a so-
> ciety, accepting its disciplines and goals. Two notions are
> thus central to the life of religions, the notions of com-
> munity and of revelation.[2]

Under the influence of Ninian Smart, Ward describes religion
as a way of life and thus comes to place Judaism in a general
context:

> It is the tradition, or Law, setting out the observances and
> prohibitions which regulate the community's inter-relations
> and its special relationship to the sacred. Tradition forms
> the basis of tribal religious life, but is rarely absent from
> the most developed religions. Many of the regulations may
> seem trivial or absurd in themselves (not to eat certain
> foods, for example), but they serve to mark off the group
> and give it a sense of identity.[3]

Viewed in this way, the Jewish doctrine of election is not
offensive but, on the contrary, a necessary manifestation of
Judaism. Its relation to Christianity can now be properly
understood:

> Part of what it means to believe in God is the participation
> in the life of a community which preserves an exemplary
> pattern of life, which may be codified in a set of rules, as
> in Judaism, or illustrated in the story of a human life, as in
> Christianity.[4]

It is, therefore, the doctrine of election–vocation of Israel
which enables us to link God, Torah and Israel into an indivisible unity and to go beyond the fragmentation caused by
the three streams of contemporary Judaism. Each of them
has, indeed, contributed to Jewish survival, and continues to
do so, but to formulate Jewish purpose a more composite

---

[2] Keith Ward, *The Concept of God* (Basil Blackwell, Oxford, 1974), p. 7.
[3] ibid., p. 9.
[4] ibid., p. 11f.

structure is required. Such a formulation requires much courage, for it exposes us to the full ferocity of anti-Semitic attacks.

25

The Greater Israel

We must be firm to impress upon the world that there is nothing exclusive in the Jewish self-understanding of election – vocation. The fact that I as a Jew regard myself as part of God's chosen people in no way implies that my Christian or Muslim neighbour is deprived of similar rights in the context of his own community, for, as Keith Ward has suggested, it is only in the life of a distinct community that belief in God becomes possible.

Everybody can be part of that community. Conversion to Judaism is no less possible than conversion to its sister-religions; in view of the growing assimilation and falling birth-rate it may be desirable. It is also a test of Jewish continuity. If Judaism has a message beyond the determination to survive, it must be made available to all who wish to have it.[1] However, although we advocate an open policy towards would-be converts, in no way do we believe that the future of Judaism depends on the influx of a large number of 'new' Jews. Too open an approach may jeopardize the distinctive characteristics of Judaism. By its very nature Judaism is a minority religion. If it were otherwise, it would have to wrestle with the problems of power and earthly domination in the way Christianity and Islam have had to do, probably with the same devastating outcome. The fact that we should open the doors to those who wish to enter, does not mean that it is our duty to engage in active missionary activity. With all the similarities between the three monotheistic religions there is a fundamental difference in this and other respects between

[1] For a fuller discussion of the question of conversion to Judaism see my *Intermarriage*, a pamphlet published by the Reform Synagogues of Great Britain.

Judaism on the one hand and Christianity and Islam on the other. The future of Judaism, therefore, cannot depend on our ability to snatch souls but on our capacity for co-existence with the other religions and our desire to work together by stressing what we have in common.

The Jewish attitude to the State is based on a consideration of the inherent tension between the potential power of the State and the real needs of individuals and of communities. It is a version of the perennial tension between Prophet and King. But the Prophetic element is not confined to Judaism but present in all religions, especially the monotheistic ones. The dimension of kingship is no longer to be sought only in the foreign State, for it is also present in the Jewish State. The need for dialogue between religion and political power is, therefore, not a purely Jewish issue, but one that concerns the world of religion as a whole. This concern points to ways of genuine co-operation across religious boundaries.

There are other factors which make such co-operation imperative. One of them is the reality that religionists in the Western world have had to identify as a common adversary: secularism. The paradigm of Jacob wrestling with the mysterious being needs now to be re-stated, for Jacob now represents not only the Jew but also everybody for whom God is a living reality. And the guardian angel of Esau is not merely the spirit of the Gentile world but also the spirit which seeks to eliminate the religious dimension from our existence. To become Israel, i.e. to wrestle a blessing out of the adversary without being destroyed by him, is no longer a purely Jewish concern but a universal religious challenge. If it is met, a greater Israel can emerge, maimed but not defeated.

That is the hope of religion in our age, but the outcome is by no means certain. The world of Jacob has been severely depleted. Christendom, which once dominated the West, has not yet adjusted to being in exile, and comprising only a small minority. Islam has not yet learnt how to take up the challenge; instead, in the manner of every strict orthodoxy, it has chosen to pretend that the challenge does not exist. As a result, despite the many beautiful words that have been spoken and the many interfaith meetings that have been held, very little real co-operation exists. The future of Judaism, indeed of all three monotheistic religions, depends, however, on such co-operation.

The Jewish component in this effort should not be underestimated. Christianity and Islam, having dominated and often persecuted Judaism for so long, are not used to reckoning with the mother religion as an equal partner. They have grown so accustomed to establishing themselves through power only that they do not believe that other methods are possible. There is still much talk in Christian and, particularly, in Islamic circles of defeating and crushing the world of secularism (and, if possible, also Judaism). Judaism, with its long experience of minority status, and its openness to God's world as it is, knows that religion is not capable of defeating secularism, and even if it could, it should not do so. For the independent critique of all aspects of human endeavour, including religion, which our secular world has made possible, has brought light into Judaism and Christianity and, in time, will do so to Islam. Had it not been for secularism, Jews would still be in the ghetto and Judaism the sole prerogative of obscurantists.

There is, therefore, no question of a battle but of dialogue, of gaining a blessing for Jacob out of the encounter with the guardian angel of Esau. Neither should we contemplate acquiescence and capitulation. The secularism of our technological world is neither the new revelation, as some Christian theologians have occasionally tried to make it out, nor is it the devil, as many conventional religionists have seen it. It is a reality, a manifestation of God's world, to which His word must address itself. Although the actual word is perceived differently by different religions – and no attempts should be made to minimize these – the basic approach is common to all. If adopted it will benefit all and, indeed, society as a whole which looks to the established religions for guidance and is dismayed when it receives either condemnation or adulation. The Prophetic corrective goes beyond both, and all who regard themselves as the disciples of the Biblical Prophets have a duty to articulate it.

In this volume an attempt has been made to formulate the nature of that corrective on the basis of Jewish tradition and Jewish experience. The point that is now being made is that the future of Judaism depends not only on its own efforts but on real understanding between the religions. It is a matter of deep regret and concern that the existing organizations for Christian–Jewish co-operation have not been able to promote such understanding to its full extent, largely due to apathy on the part of both Christians and Jews.

The lack of serious dialogue between Christians and Jews is not only jeopardizing the future of Judaism, but it is also harmful to Christianity. To start with, Christianity needs Judaism for its self-understanding, and secondly, it needs the Jewish experience of growth and development in the face of adversity and irrespective of its minority status. The fundamental differences between the two religions will and should remain; nothing has been done to conceal them in this book. But that need not prevent the real opportunity for co-operation that also exists. Its basis is once again tension: tension between Judaism and Christianity and tension between the monotheistic religions on the one hand and secularism on the other. To exist and even flourish in that tension by testifying to God's presence in the world is a sign of true chosenness, real belonging to a world-wide community of the faithful. It is impossible to imagine a future for Judaism, or for its sister religions, without the tension and the testimony.

VII

THE HOPE OF RENEWAL

*Waiting for the Beyond whilst Living in the
Here and Now*

Wherever people work to produce something, wherever they cultivate the fields,
wherever they marry, wherever they found
and raise families, wherever they learn or
teach, wherever they engage in political
activities, there is hope. For in all these
activities and in a host of others that have not
been mentioned, there is an affirmation of the
future, a trust in the future, an investment in
the future.

John Macquarrie[1]

---

[1] John Macquarrie, *Christian Hope* (Mowbray 1978), p. 4.

26

The Wisdom of Insecurity[1]

The quotation from John Macquarrie on the previous page sums up the faith that has prompted the writing of this book. It is also an apt, albeit unconscious, paraphrase of Jeremiah's message to the exiles in Babylonia.

By trying to describe the prospects of Jewish life in terms of work and family life, learning and response to political realities, I have tried to point to the future of Judaism, not as a soothsayer, but as a teacher of Jewish tradition indicating what *ought* to happen rather than what *will* happen. Characteristically, the quotation is taken from a book on Christian theology, not because I share the author's religious convictions but because I subscribe to his method. This book is intended as a modest manifestation of the belief in the possibility of a common understanding between exponents of Judaism and Christianity in the face of a world whose leading intellectual figures have sought to encourage us 'to live without hope'.

That the issue is wider than Jewish–Christian co-operation is reflected in the heading of this section. It is the title of a book by Alan W. Watts, which by implication challenges the notion of hopelessness by pointing the way to living with insecurity. And Watts' religious concerns go beyond the confines of any established religion and yet encompass many of them. He calls his book 'a message for an age of anxiety'. We must listen to it with care: it is a compelling alternative both to the life of insecurity caused by anti-Semitism and to the insecurity of the fatherless, both of which have been discussed earlier in this volume.

Watts accepts the insecurity which, in our scheme of things,

[1] I have published an article with the same title, comprising – albeit in a different form – the first section of this chapter, in *European Judaism*, xi, 1 (Winter 1976/7), p. 16ff.

is the inevitable corollary to our need to encounter repeatedly
'the guardian angel of Esau'. But what makes that insecurity
bearable is the 'belief in unchanging things beyond the reach
of calamity – in God, in man's immortal soul, and in the
government of the universe by eternal laws of right'.[2] As the
faith in these values decreases in the world it becomes more
necessary than ever for Jews, Christians and other believers
to testify to them.

Inevitably, the testimony will be mingled with insecurity.
Too often religionists have opted for the safety of the veneration of the past in place of the dangers of the affirmation of
the present, but in so doing they have offered knowledge
where wisdom has been required, and invoked history,
dogma, law instead of making room for real experience. For
wisdom, according to Watts, '. . . is not factual knowledge
nor mere quantity and range of experience, nor even facility
in the use of knowledge and experience. Wisdom is a quality
of the psychological or spiritual relationship between man and
his experience. When that relationship is wise and harmonious
man's experiences set him free, but when it is unwise and
discordant his experiences bind him.'[3]

Watts believed that 'religion alone can deal with that relationship, and this is its essential function'.[4] Apparently he did
not find religion in the Judaeo–Christian tradition and sought
it elsewhere. His search was obviously sufficiently important
for many because he became something of a cult-figure. But
is really such wisdom beyond the scope of the Judaeo–Christian tradition? It is not for me to speak for Christianity, but
do not our Jewish Scriptures speak of it, and have not our
sages taught it? Is not it only the narrow quest for survival
that has made it impossible for us to engage in dialogue with
the world and to accept what we know in our bones, namely
that 'there *is* no safety or security',[5] and that 'running away
from fear is fear, fighting pain is pain, trying to be brave is
being scared'?[6]

[2] Alan W. Watts, *The Wisdom of Insecurity* (Pantheon, New York, 1951),
p. 16.
[3] Alan W. Watts, *The Meaning of Happiness* (Village Press, London, 1968),
p. 50.
[4] ibid.
[5] *The Wisdom of Insecurity*, p. 79.
[6] ibid., p. 97.

The Jewish quest for survival has, understandably, placed us all in the grip of fear. We look at the statistics of assimilation, at low birth-rate and intermarriage in the Western Diaspora, and we fear that even American Jewry will not survive. We look at the political situation in the Middle East, and the prospects of the Jewish State, and we are scared. As a result, most things that we do as Jews tend to be motivated by the overriding desire to counteract the dangers of annihilation from without and the risk of erosion from within. Instead of engaging 'the guardian angel of Esau' in a combat, we take evasive action in the hope that the adversary will go away. Instead of combining forces with our Christian neighbours, whose minority status now more and more resembles the Jewish condition, we insist on separation, even isolation. The irony is, of course, that the very people we wish to 'save' for Judaism often turn away from us to join teachers like Alan Watts, because his message offers a prospect for the future by dealing with the problems of the present.

Concern with the present is another characteristic of 'the wisdom of insecurity'. Whereas the quest for safety and survival retreats into the past in order to 'secure' the future, the search for wisdom is primarily concerned with the here and now. That is the true nature of religion; it is when it becomes 'scientific' and puts history and statistics in place of love and experience that it retreats into the past or dreams about the future. In all such situations the present is shunned and things to come are imagined as a complete break with what there is now. Instead of growth we get revolution; instead of realistic hope we get empty optimism.

Significantly, both Rosenzweig and Buber saw the essence of religious life in the response in the here and now. Neither observance for Rosenzweig nor love born out of dialogue for Buber can be stored; it has to be lived and experienced in the present. God Himself becomes known to Moses as *Ehyeh-Asher-Ehyeh* (*Exodus* 3:14) which the Buber–Rosenzweig Bible translation renders as 'I am the Ever Present'. The God of Abraham, Isaac and Jacob is first and foremost *Eloheynu*, our God, here and now, if we are to heed His call and worship Him.

It is not a secure existence, and the future it offers is an uncertain one, but it is the only possible way of living. Moses received his call in the wilderness and did not know whether he would ever reach the Promised Land, but his response at the Burning Bush was nevertheless *Hineni*, 'Here I am' (*Exodus* 3:4). And the fact that he himself did not reach the Promised Land in no way invalidated his endeavours; his successor completed what he had started.

There is no movement in contemporary Judaism that has been able to adopt this philosophy. Orthodoxy is by its very nature wedded to the past. Zionist ideology has become increasingly so; its revolutionary fervour is now more and more directed towards vindicating the territorial claims by the Biblical authors. Even Reform, originator of a new perception of Judaism, has now become imprisoned in its 150-year-old history and in its powerful institutions. The veneration of the past, or of the land, or of buildings and projects has made 'necrophiliacs' of all of us.

In order to love the living and not the dead we have to open ourselves to the call for wisdom as enunciated by Watts and many others. That is a universal need on the part of the monotheistic religions of the West.

As far as Judaism is concerned, insecurity is endemic to Jewish life and the most obvious response to it in recent times has been the struggle for survival. But that struggle is self-defeating and, by some strange irony, it may even exacerbate the dangers. As an alternative, based on the experience of Judaism through the ages, living with insecurity seems to be more indigenous to our tradition and part of our purpose as Jews. By being totally exposed to what human power can inflict on us, we have to rely completely on the power of God. To do so is to have trust in God, which is stronger than mere faith in Him. Through our scepticism and reserve toward earthly kingdoms we are better able to keep the Kingdom of God in focus.

There is a heavy price to be paid for living with insecurity, and after the Holocaust it became quite obvious that we Jews could not go on paying it without, at least, a respite. The creation of the State of Israel was absolutely necessary for our continued existence. Its creation, and the sovereignty that came with it, gave Jews access to power. There seemed no longer the same urgency to wait for the heavenly Jerusalem, because the earthly Jerusalem was within reach. Insecurity was no longer the heritage of Israel because the soldiers of the State that bore its name could provide security, *bittachon*. Israel had at last emerged with a real blessing; he may still have been maimed and limping but he was saved with prospects for triumph over all his foes.

The Hebrew word, *bittachon*, now used as the term for military 'security', started off as a theological term and meant 'trust'. It sought to express the feeling that the Biblical Isaac had towards his father on their way to Moriah, as a reflection of the feeling that Abraham had for God, our heavenly Father. It is the secularization of this word which epitomizes the burden of contemporary Jewry.

We are not entitled to castigate the Israelis for having changed the meaning. History forced it upon them, upon us all. Without their valiant defence of the Jewish homeland, few Jews would have wished to continue to live, let alone to believe. Nevertheless, without the return to its original connotation – but not, God forbid, by jeopardizing the security of the State of Israel – the future of Judaism seems, to say the least, improbable. Judaism was founded on trust; therefore it can never exist on mere security. Trust is a daring expression; the trusting Abraham and Isaac walked towards Moriah in 'fear and trembling', in great insecurity, but also in true wisdom.

The mixture of martyrdom and heroism that has been characteristic of Jews in this century appears to have made us invincible. We responded to the massacres of the Nazis and the machinations of the Arabs with determination and amazing strength. However, in order to be victorious we cannot rely merely on our own resources; for that, trust in God is needed. The way to such trust is linked to the wisdom that comes from insecurity.

The State of Israel presents us Jews with a great opportunity, but it also brings with it great dangers. I am not referring to the political complications, but to the real risk that the new generation of Jews, in Israel and elsewhere, will confuse security with trust and, worse still, abandon the latter. Events in recent years in Israel suggest that the risks can be contained and that the religious heritage need not be squandered. To strengthen all forces which work on behalf of, and in the spirit of, trust has become a priority for all Jews.

Maybaum's message to the new generation, warning against the lethal mixture of nationalism and religion, must be heeded:

> The Jew can hail the Jewish State as a precious gift granted to him. He can be a citizen and can be a soldier after the fashion of Greek antiquity. Yet the Jew must not become reduced to what citizens and soldiers are. They are lifted to the tragic realm of the spirit which constitutes both State and Church. Prophetic Judaism's double task of affirmation and negation presents itself here. We must say 'yes', and we must know when to say 'no'. A politicized and spiritualized Judaism – Jews entirely and exclusively characterized as citizens and soldiers – is not the Judaism to which prophetic Judaism aspires.[7]

Non-Jews can, of course, make their special contribution here. If Islam can contain its militancy and stress its sense of tolerance and brotherhood, which it also possesses, the pressures on Israel would ease and with it the emphasis on security. That is why the peace treaty with Egypt, despite all the drawbacks and difficulties, has such deep *religious* implications.

Israel cannot exist without coming to terms with the Arab world, and the Arab world is identified with Islam as much as Israel is identified with Judaism. There, an encounter between the two religions is needed; it is difficult to envisage the future of Judaism without it. But there is very little to suggest that Islam is ready for dialogue. According to Professor Bernard Lewis,[8] 'Islam from its inception is a religion of power, and in the Muslim world view it is right and proper that power should be wielded by Muslims and Muslims alone'. He quotes the saying, current in the Arab world before the 1967 Arab–Israeli War, 'First the Saturday people, then the Sunday people'. In the light of repeated threats to the existence of Israel by the Palestine Liberation Organization (PLO) and the vast majority of Arab states supporting it, the threat must be taken for what it is. Events in Iran, Lebanon and elsewhere suggest that Christians, and indeed the West as a

---

[7] Ignaz Maybaum, *Trialogue between Jew, Christian and Muslim* (Routledge & Kegan Paul 1973), p. 170.

[8] 'The Return of Islam' in *Commentary*, January 1976.

whole, is in grave danger. The fact that Western states do not seem to realize it and, for the sake of short-term gains, support the PLO further compounds the problem.

It would of course be ludicrous to contemplate a military campaign to annihilate Islam. We must learn to live with it. Christians and Jews, the 'greater Israel', must wrestle with the spirit of Islam and struggle to extract a blessing from it. The principle of dialogue must also include this encounter.

The reason for the difficulty to do so is, of course, linked to the fact that Islamic militancy has often found its ally in Communism, as reflected in the political situation in the Middle East. Whatever the cynical reasons for the alliance, it is a reality and, what is more, the power of Communism is a reality too. We did not need Solzhenitsyn to be reminded of it, but there is little doubt that his testimony has alerted the world to the menace of Communism.

But as ludicrous and as dangerous as it would be to seek to defeat Islam on the battlefield, so it would be had we attempted to destroy the Communist empire. Unpalatable though it may seem, co-existence is the only viable alternative and once again the wrestling Jacob comes to mind. Christianity has already made some attempts to come to terms with Communist–Marxist ideology and Judaism has to learn from it and to join forces. There is thus more than one Jabbok at which Israel's resourcefulness is to be tested. The insecurity is understandable, but wisdom dictates that we must take the risks and trust.

It has been the peculiar destiny of the Jews to encounter both militant Islam and imperialist Communism in the struggle for the survival of the State of Israel. The situation is further complicated by the fact that both have been formative influences on the Jewish State. Thus about half of Israel's population has its roots in the Islamic world and has, in so many ways, been influenced by it. At the same time, the pioneers of Israel were often motivated by the same ideas as the Russian revolutionaries. Israel has already extracted something of the blessing of both Islam and Communism; the Jewish world must now find a way of completing the process. If it succeeds – *when* it succeeds – it will have shown the whole Western world how it can be done. Once again a Jewish particularist concern may have universal implications.

How the encounter is to take place in practice is difficult to say, although there has been no lack of initiatives to engage Egyptian intellectuals in dialogue as soon as the peace treaty with their country was signed. Neither have attempts been lacking to build bridges with the Communist world, when contacts were possible; the relationship between Israel and Romania to this very day is significant and important. What is needed is the basic will and the ability to create and take opportunities. By seeing Judaism as a bridge-builder we define for it yet another role in the future, yet another dimension of its purpose.

27

Wisdom and Knowledge

The external threat to Israel, epitomized by the combined efforts of Islamic militancy and Communist imperialism, has a universalist dimension. The way the Jews come to terms with the problem may be a paradigm for the world, if peace is to be preserved: the paradigm of Jacob wrestling with the guardian angel of Esau to become Israel gains a new significance in this context. The question now to be asked is: can Diaspora Jewry come to terms with its external foe, anti-Semitism, in a similar fashion? Can the narrow quest for survival from persecution be turned into a broad purpose of co-operation and mutual enrichment?

Experience has shown that factual information and logical argument do not eradicate anti-Semitism. The study of collective psychopathology may help us to understand the problem, but there is no real indication that it helps us to solve it. Therefore, the only possible alternative would be a combined effort to identify and remove the main causes of anti-Semitism. In the same way as hatred of the black minorities, reflected in the periodic ascendance of extremist right-wing groups in the Americas and in Europe, will not be removed merely by education, or even legislation, but by the alleviation of the social and economic conditions that exacerbate it, so the hatred of Jews can only be diminished through a similar attention to causes.

Our limited knowledge in this field is enough to suggest that anti-Semitism is brought about by the unwise response to insecurity. The Christian, whether still believing or already secularized, facing the threat to his existence as a human being and as a member of a group, panics and looks for a scapegoat. The Jew is the obvious target, accepted by tradition. If the Jew is to continue to live side by side with his

Gentile neighbour, i.e. if the Diaspora is to continue, we must seek to turn the foolish search for scapegoats into a search for wisdom. And even if Jews should disappear from the West, the way they have already disappeared from Eastern Europe and the Arab countries, the search for wisdom will still be paramount, unless other minority groups are to become the new Jews. The suggestion made earlier in this book that there exists a kind of sick collusion between anti-Semite and Jew must now be turned into co-operation between Jew and Gentile in a common search for wisdom. Instead of defending ourselves so that we might survive, we must seek to influence the society in which we live so that it, and we in it, might survive.

This task is currently thwarted in the Western world by the profound and devastating confusion between wisdom and knowledge. E. F. Schumacher described the former as 'science for understanding' and the latter as 'science for manipulation':

> The 'science for understanding' saw man as made in the image of God, the crowning glory of creation, and hence 'in charge' of the world, because *noblesse oblige*. The 'science for manipulation', inevitably, sees man as nothing but an accidental product of evolution, a higher animal, a social animal, and an object for study by the same methods by which other phenomena of this world were to be studied – 'objectively'. Wisdom is a type of knowledge that can be used only by bringing into play the highest and noblest powers of the mind; 'science for manipulation', by contrast, is a type of knowledge that can be used by bringing into play only such powers as are possessed by everybody except the severely handicapped, mainly pointer reading and counting, without any need to understand why a formula works: to know that it *does* work is enough for practical and manipulative purposes.[1]

Therefore, according to Schumacher, 'the progressive elimination of "science for understanding" – or "wisdom" – in Western civilisation turns the rapid and ever accelerating

---

[1] E. F. Schumacher, *A Guide for the Perplexed* (Jonathan Cape 1977), p. 65f.

accumulation of "knowledge for manipulation" into a most serious threat'.[2]

In an earlier book Schumacher had asserted that 'man is far too clever to be able to survive without wisdom'. He wrote then:

> The hope that the pursuit of goodness and virtue can be postponed until we have attained universal prosperity and that by the single-minded pursuit of wealth, without bothering our heads about spiritual and moral questions, we could establish peace on earth, is an unrealistic, unscientific, and irrational hope. The exclusion of wisdom from economics, science, and technology was something which we would perhaps get away with for a little while, as long as we were relatively unsuccessful; but now that we have become very successful, the problem of spiritual and moral truth moves into the central position.[3]

Schumacher's distinction between *understanding* and *manipulation*, between wisdom and knowledge, is akin to Fromm's juxtaposition of *being* and *having*. Both imply that modern technology has objectified the world, that – in Buber's terminology – we can only relate on an *I–it* basis to it, whereas what is needed is an *I–thou* relationship to the world around us. What is significant is that it is not suggested that the world of *manipulation*, of *having* and of *it*, should be negated, but that for man to make proper use of the world of objects, he has to relate to them in a different way.

The situation is likely to become more acute as technology advances. A British professor, referred to earlier in this book, submitted a few years ago a paper to his Government in which he stated that 'it must become the priority of government, industry and the trade unions to effect the orderly transfer of labour from the manufacturing to the knowledge industries. The logical way to accomplish this is by means of huge expansion in the education system'.[4] The recommendation is a characteristic manifestation of secular thinking. It compares

---

[2] ibid., p. 66.
[3] E. F. Schumacher, *Small is Beautiful* (Abacus 1974), p. 26.
[4] *The Times*, London, 13 November 1978, reporting on a working paper submitted to the British Government's 'Think Tank' by Professor Tom Stonier of Bradford University. See Part V. p. 138.

manufacturing to knowledge and believes that both are capable of industrialization. The calculation about the future is a matter of 'orderly transfer of labour'. It recommends *having* knowledge when what is required is *being* wise, seemingly ignoring the fact that the former is only likely to produce more frustration, anxiety and insecurity, turning the dream of a life of leisure into a nightmare of a life of crime and violence. The production and acquisition of facts only adds to the problem, whereas the growth of wisdom offers a genuine solution.

That such wisdom leads to 'holy insecurity' has already been considered in this chapter. The fact that wisdom does not negate knowledge but seeks to transform it, wrestle with it for the sake of authenticity, makes for continued uncertainty. Acquisition of facts, by contrast, makes for false security and a new kind of dogmatism.

Judaism has its access to wisdom in Torah and by seeking to relate its tradition to the world – in a constant tension between the timeless and the timely; it makes for personal involvement and renewal, for a state of *being*, for a relationship of dialogue. The force of Torah has been described in an earlier chapter of this book, as has its significance for the growth of leisure in the age of technology. Diaspora Jewry is in a position to testify to the power of this approach – without in any way wishing to impose its content – as an indication that the problems of our time cannot be solved only, or perhaps even primarily, by officials in 'government, industry and the trade unions' but by genuine teachers.

Walter Kaufmann has suggested that the combination of passion for justice and love of learning is uniquely Jewish.[5] Jewish Diaspora existence, in addition to its particularist tasks, also has the universalist dimension of testimony. By combining the love of learning with the love of man, it makes for subjective knowledge, wisdom, as a corrective to the 'acquisition of pure knowledge for the sake of manipulation'.

Although there is much to suggest that Jews have been in the forefront of both the pursuit of learning and the pursuit

---

[5] See, for example, Walter Kaufmann's essay 'The Future of Jewish Identity' in his *Existentialism, Religion and Death* (New American Library 1976), p. 164 ff. Kaufmann also includes the love of music and literature in what he describes as the *Kaufmann syndrome*.

of social justice, the Jewish community as a whole has tended to succumb to the world of manipulation and *having*. Significantly, many of those who have wished to fulfil the Prophetic ideal of justice, combined with the Rabbinic ideal of learning, have often had to do so outside the community, even in opposition to it. The future of Judaism must, therefore, entail a drastic re-evaluation of community structure in order to allow for a new openness. The Jewish community must see its purpose in the context of society as a whole, not merely in terms of its own continuity and survival.

The absence of a community life based on Torah and social justice leads to anxiety. Western society illustrates it; continued anti-Semitism within it is a symptom of its disease. The resources inherent in the faith of Israel can turn that anxiety into trust and hope. To do so it will need the co-operation of the Church and active confrontation with the secular forces in our society. God, Torah and Israel provide, on the one hand, the particularist vision of Judaism and, on the other, the universalist vision of religion in the West. The possible interaction between the two opens new possibilities for the 'greater Israel' even though it may be naïve to assume that a Jewish interest in dialogue will eradicate, or even diminish, anti-Semitism. And yet, it is only on that assumption that hope becomes possible for Gentile and Jew alike.

Insecurity that is not fear and wisdom that is more than knowledge are also two basic factors that make for hope. John Macquarrie makes the point that fear on its own is the very negation of hope[6] and what passes as knowledge is frequently inimical to hope, 'for what is the point of putting any energy into one's actions if one is already persuaded that things will turn out one way or the other in any case?'[7] Only by recognizing the limitations to both security and knowledge do we create the possibilities for genuine hope.

This, in turn, points to the ambiguity of the world in which we live, because 'hope is possible only in an ambiguous world, a world in which all is not utterly bad and yet one in which nothing is perfect either'. Echoing Edmond Fleg's declaration, 'I am a Jew because, for Israel, the world is not yet

[6] Macquarrie, op cit., p. 6.
[7] ibid., p. 9.

completed: men are completing it,' [8] Macquarrie adds: 'This would, of course, be the case in an unfinished world where creation is still going on and in which man is summoned to play a responsible part in the creative process.' [9]

The Jewish thinker to take the most courageous consequences of this understanding of hope was the late Ignaz Maybaum. His statement may have been made ahead of his time, when the Jewish world was not yet ready to see the Holocaust in the perspective of hope, but it may also turn out to be truly Prophetic. In an interview in connection with his seventieth birthday[10] he drew the important distinction between hope and calculation and pleaded against the latter in this post-Holocaust era. Auschwitz was for him not only 'the great trial' when 'the Jew is tried, tested, like Abraham at Moriah' and 'those after Auschwitz who still believe in God, His justice and His mercy, are the right Jews, the remnant', but he also saw hope in the midst of the tragedy. Although he pleaded, 'You must not force me to specify my hopes,' he also said:

> . . . what has happened might have been the price we had to pay for the collapse of the untenable feudalism of Eastern Europe. There was an historic necessity to break down the system and the holocaust did it . . . after a thousand years of German oppression the Slavs are now free. The Oder–Neisse line denotes progress. I could also say that the Ashkenazi, European, diaspora has become a world diaspora. That too is progress.

Offensive though his words may seem to camp survivors, they may nevertheless denote a fundamental truth, which unfolds itself in contemporary history, manifest, for example, in the struggle for freedom in Poland. By describing the Holocaust as *churban* (destruction), a term used in Jewish tradition for the destruction of both the First Temple and the Second Temple in Biblical times, Maybaum sees it, with great hesitation and almost reluctantly, in the same historic context.

---

[8] Edmond Fleg, *Why I am a Jew* (Victor Gollancz 1943), p. 61. See Part V, p. 139.

[9] Macquarrie, op. cit., p. 13.

[10] 'Maybaum at Seventy' in *Living Judaism*, Journal of the Reform Synagogues of Great Britain, i, 3 (Spring 1967), p. 72f.

As the Babylonian Exile, for all the pain it caused, denotes progress in Jewish history, and as the devastation by the Romans in 70 CE enabled Judaism to grow even though Jewry was decimated, so the destruction in our own times, for all its unspeakable devastation, is, almost paradoxically, an opportunity for hope. The Prophets saw even Nebuchadnezzar as God's tool, and the Rabbis viewed Vespasian and Titus as divine instruments.

The Jewish propensity to hope has been recognized by Jürgen Moltmann who, for all his Christological stance, is able to appreciate the significance of the Biblical notion of covenant, which consists of both promise and command.[11] Providing Israel keeps the command, God will fulfil the promise, providing Abraham does God's will and submits to the test at Moriah, God will make him into a great nation. Hope is thus assured to everyone who wills it. The wisdom of insecurity is manifest in the readiness to act according to God's command in the face of the obvious danger. And for such action, neither calculation nor a grasp of the relevant facts is sufficient.

> The world is not yet finished, but is understood as engaged in a history. It is therefore the world of possibilities, the world in which we can serve the future, promised truth and righteousness and peace. This is an age of diaspora, of sowing in hope, of self-surrender and sacrifice, for it is an age which stands within the horizon of a new future. Thus self-expenditure in this world, day-to-day love in hope, becomes possible and becomes human within that horizon of expectation which transcends this world.[12]

Such hope expresses itself, *inter alia*, in equal emphasis on past, present and future. Macquarrie has written that 'Israel finds its identity both by committing itself to a future and by accepting its past, and understands its present in the light of

---

[11] See also Macquarrie, *op. cit* p. 37: 'It is important to notice too that from the beginning the messianic hope or expectation was a dialectical one. It depended upon a promise or covenant by which God had committed himself to his people, but the people too had their responsibility arising from the covenant, and they had to fulfil that responsibility if the promise was to be realized.'

[12] Jürgen Moltmann, *Theology of Hope* (SCM 1969), p. 338.

both'.[13] My critique of the three movements in contemporary Judaism is partly based on the grounds that none of them has been able to create the necessary balance for the finding of Israel's identity in our time. Orthodoxy has been too pre-occupied with the past, with revelation rather than with promise (as Moltmann puts it); Zionism has been obsessed with the present, overstressing short-term political gains at the expense of long-term aims for the benefit of all Jews and Judaism as a whole; Reform has invested more in the future, in promise rather than in revelation, and thus alienated its adherents from the sources of Judaism and estranged them from the political realities that threaten Jewish survival. My grounds for optimism (which, as Macquarrie points out, is not to be confused with hope) are founded on the measure of self-criticism currently in evidence in all three camps and on the prospect of a genuine coming together, the possibility of a Judaism that transcends denominational divisions and yet contains the tensions and the differences.

[13] Macquarrie, op. cit., p. 46.

28

The Next Phase

Whether the optimism and the hope are warranted or not will depend on the nature of the next phase of contemporary Judaism. In this way we will best respond to Kaufmann's challenge, to which reference has been made in the Preface, to concentrate on what to do next. Reviewing the development of Reform Judaism, Gunther Plaut[1] suggests that it is now moving into a new phase, which may be more open to the possibility of dialogue than has been the case hitherto. And what is true of Reform may also be applicable to Zionism, and even to Orthodoxy.

According to Plaut, the first phase of Reform, in the early days of its existence, tried to address itself to the question, 'What does Tradition say?' The founders wanted to justify their actions in the eyes of the past. In the second phase, once Reform was established, especially in America, 'the demands, the ideologies and the opportunities of the environment were dominant'. It was a time when being accepted by the Gentiles was of primary importance because through such acceptance emancipation was to be vindicated. The third phase was pre-occupied with the question, 'What will my children say?' According to Plaut, with the advent of Hitler, 'the issue had now shifted away from the environment and its culture to the issue of survival'. By 1965 Reform had entered a fourth phase when personal experience became the paramount concern in America and elsewhere and Jewish modernists were influenced by it. The 1980s, writes Plaut, may see the emergence of yet another phase. He dare not forecast what it will be, but writes: 'I know what I would like it to be. I would like it to

[1] W. Gunther Plaut, 'Reform Judaism: Past, Present and Future', in *Journal of Reform Judaism*, published by the Central Conference of American Rabbis, xxvii, 3 (Summer 1980), p. 1ff.

respond to the urgent question *mah yomru bameromim*? "What do they say on high?" '. In the terminology applied throughout this book, the next phase will mean the renewal of the encounter that transformed Jacob into Israel.

Plaut believes that an attempt to describe the next phase would enable Reform Judaism to 'move into a period where its impact on Jewish life would match the splendour of its early years and would give a new face to its meaning and thrust'. The attempt in this book to describe the necessary tension in an integrated view of Judaism – in which our vision of God, our understanding of His word and our membership of His people are in the same mould – is intended as a contribution to the answer to Plaut's fifth question. The answer has to be tentative and halting, for as Plaut himself puts it:

> Meanwhile, however, we are suspended between the after-effects of the 1960s and the anticipation of 1984. We search within, at least tentatively, but we do not wish to give up on our potential impact on the world. We are not certain of ourselves, and that in itself is no shortcoming. We are at this moment a movement in search. Perhaps we will indeed be blessed by the challenge and promise of the prophet: *Dirshu Adonai b'himatzo* (Seek the Lord while He can be found, *Isaiah* 55:6).

We are suspended, partly at least, due to the fact that one phase does not succeed another as neatly as Plaut, the historian, would have it. In reality all his five phases exist side by side, and not only in Reform Judaism but in the other modernist movements too. Orthodoxy and Zionism too are anxious to explain and justify themselves in the eyes of tradition; to appear modern and relevant to current ideas and ideologies; to safeguard Judaism for future generations; to offer a way to personal fulfilment; to claim authenticity by the demands of 'on high'. Contemporary Judaism, whether Orthodox, Reform or Zionist, struggles to make tradition meaningful; to make it possible for the Jew to live in the modern world; to transmit the teachings to the next generation; to present these teachings in ways that make for personal experience; to strive for authenticity. The fact that they fail has to do with the ideologies on which they have been founded.

They are now being urged to change their basic assumptions in order to realize better their avowed aims.

To me, the movement that has the best prospect of bringing about the necessary change is Reform Judaism, especially as it is evolving in Britain, where it is showing remarkable affinities to American Reform and American Conservative Judaism. It can thus act as a bridge between them and serve as a model for Reform–Conservative Judaism in Israel. British Reform is open to the stress on tradition as manifest in Orthodoxy, but without the latter's fundamentalist stance and legalistic extremism. It remains open to the influences of the non-Jewish world, but without the lapses into a kind of Unitarianism manifest in some Jewish liberal circles. It is passionately concerned with Jewish education, and now fully recognizes the force of Zionism and Israel in these endeavours, and yet it refuses to shut out the world from Jewish consciousness. It pays attention to the yearning for religious experience but without the extremism of the Chasidim. And it is perhaps more determined to reach Plaut's next phase than any other movement in Judaism today.

To work within such a framework can easily lead to self-contradiction, for the ideal can never be realized and compromise becomes inevitable. Religious life thus becomes a continuous struggle and a constant taking of risks: if you seek to banish Satan with Satan you are likely to be left with Satan in the end; practical involvement in Jewish life leaves me, therefore, exposed and vulnerable. But not to take the risks reduces me to inactivity that borders on irresponsibility and to futile Messianic expectation. That is why vacillation between particularism and universalism, Priestly realism and Prophetic fervour, is the price I pay in my effort to come a little closer to the next phase. My quest for purpose does not exclude my pre-occupation with survival, in the same way as Fackenheim's imperative to survive does not ignore other issues:

If the 614th commandment [to survive] is binding upon the authentic Jew, then we are, first, commanded to survive as Jews, lest the Jewish people perish. We are commanded, second, to remember in our very guts and bones the martyrs of the Holocaust, lest their memory perish. We are forbidden, thirdly, to deny or despair of God, however much we may have to contend with Him or with belief in Him, lest Judaism perish. We are forbidden, finally, to despair of the world as the place which is to become the kingdom of God, lest we help make it a meaningless place in which God is dead or irrelevant and everything is permitted.[2]

Fackenheim's four-fold commandment is evenly divided between the specifically Jewish and the universal. Even his near-obsession with the Holocaust and its martyrs does not permit him to despair of God and the world. In a sense, this book is a gloss on Fackenheim's formula, for before Jacob could encounter 'the guardian angel of Esau' he had to seek protection in exile, and before he could wrestle with God at Peniel he had to contend with the seemingly mundane pursuits of providing for his family.

The seven answers of the Preface to the question, 'Why Judaism?' can now be re-formulated, allowing for modifications that contain something of a programme for the future. For our concern is not only with why we should stay Jewish but also with why our children should wish to be Jews. Despite their limited scope these answers may enable us to face the challenge of the world as it moves towards the close of the twentieth century, through purposeful action rather than idle speculation:

1. We are links in the chain of a remarkable history, but *we must not become slaves to the past*. Knowledge of tradition may lead to veneration, but wisdom will give us the courage to reject its dictates if they are contrary to the needs and aspirations of the present. The past has no right to impede the future.

2. As Jews we understand pain, our own and that of others, but *that does not entitle us to despair*. Hope is possible even in the midst of catastrophe. The Prophet's vision of the dry bones that came to life again (*Ezekiel* 37) and the Psalmist's assertion, 'You turned my lament into dancing' (*Psalms* 30:12) are part of ancient history and current experience.

3. To be Jewish is to be *witness to the world, not to evoke its sense of guilt but to show a way to repentance*. In our universalist

[2] Emil L. Fackenheim, 'Jewish Values in the Post-Holocaust Future', in *Judaism*, xvi, 3 (Summer 1967), p. 272f.

emphasis we are, with Fackenheim, forbidden 'to despair of the world as the place which is to become the kingdom of God, lest we help make it a meaningless place'.

4. Judaism shows us *a way to God, not through blind obedience but in genuine dialogue.* Man's 'coming of age' has not rendered God 'dead or irrelevant' but has alerted man to his true potential as God's partner who, like Israel, finds his true identity in wrestling with God.

5. Judaism gives us access to a unique source of wisdom, but *a wisdom that must be shared with the world.* Torah is the specific heritage of Israel, but it is also God's blueprint for the world.

6. As Jews we are part of a world-wide community of Jews, but *we live in a world of Gentiles.* The covenant at Sinai, like the struggle at Peniel beckons us all, if we are willing to pay the price.

7. Judaism is a source of hope, *both as Messianic speculation and as a way of life* through which God's promise is fulfilled.

Although the above modifications to the original seven answers may appear slight, they are nevertheless essential, for they help us to know what to do next. The next phase has a lofty purpose, but it is not a utopian dream and, therefore, it can be reached through a realistic programme of action, which in no way diminishes the necessary stress on Jewish survival and yet seeks to go beyond it. While the Israelites were still Pharaoh's slaves in Egypt, Moses and Aaron were already legislating, giving seemingly trivial instructions, for what was to happen in the Promised Land,[3] for they knew that the future had already started. It is still with us and only by taking one step at a time can we inherit it.

[3] See *Exodus* 12:14ff.

Glossary of Hebrew Terms

Avodah 'Service', both in the sense of work and worship. Prayer is described in Rabbinic literature as service of the heart.

Ba'al teshuvah (pl. *ba'aley teshuvah*) 'He who repents'. A term used nowadays to describe assimilated Jews who have been 'born again' by 'returning' to strict Orthodox practice.

Barmitsvah (fem. *Batmitsvah*) 'Son of the commandment' ('daughter of the commandment'). Based on the Jewish traditional notion that when boys reach the age of 13 (and girls the age of 12), they become responsible for their own actions in the eyes of God.

Bittachon 'Trust' and 'security', used theologically in the former sense and politically in the latter.

Chasidism (adj. *chasidic*) A movement which started among Jews in eighteenth century Eastern Europe stressing piety and learning. The word *chasid* means 'pious'.

Chatan (pl. *chatanim*) 'Bridegroom'.

Chavurah (pl. *chavurot*) 'Fellowship'. Used in contemporary Jewish life to describe groups of Jews who meet for worship and study, frequently outside the conventional Synagogue structure.

Chutspah 'Insolence'.

Din 'Law', usually in the sense of 'verdict', describing not so much the process as the concensus of codifiers and judges that makes for normative Orthodox practice.

Elohim 'God'.

Erets 'Land' and 'earth'.

Halacha (adj. *halachic*) 'Law' denoting the process of discussing and establishing the practical teachings of Jewish tradition. *Halachic* decisions make for *din*.

Hasidism see *Chasidism*

Hatikvah Lit. 'hope'. the national anthem of the State of Israel and, by implication, of the Jewish people.

Kabbalah 'That which has been received'. The technical term for the mystical tradition in Judaism.

Kadosh 'Holy'.

Kol Nidre Lit. 'all vows'. The first two words of the opening prayer recited in the Synagogue on the eve of the Day of Atonement, which have given the name to the evening as a whole.

Kosher Religiously fit as viewed by Orthodoxy.

Masoretic text The printed and vocalised standard text of the Hebrew Bible. The Hebrew word *masora* means 'tradition'.

Meah Shearim Lit. 'a hundred gates'. A district in Jerusalem where some of the city's most Orthodox inhabitants live.

Medinah 'State'.

Menorah 'Lampstand' – especially the seven branched candlestick, one of the oldest symbols of Judaism.

Metsaveh 'Commander'. Used also as a synonym for God the Lawgiver.

Midrash 'Exegesis'. The genre of Rabbinic literature of homilies, legends and other interpretations of Biblical texts.

Minhag 'Custom'.

Mishnah 'Teaching'. The collective name of the 63 tractates, divided into six main sections, which constitute an authoritative record of Jewish teaching, particularly in the realm of *Halacha*, at the time of its compilation, around 200 CE.

Mitsvah (pl. mitsvot) 'Commandment' with special reference to the will of God, as understood by Jewish tradition, to be performed by the Jew.

Rabbi 'My teacher'. The technical term used to describe the religious leader of a congregation of Jews. The title can only be bestowed by other rabbis following a thorough examination of the candidate's knowledge of all aspects of Jewish tradition.

Rabbinic literature is another name for *Mishnah*, *Midrash* and *Talmud*.

Rashi Abbreviation of *Rabbi Shlomo Itzchaki* of Troyes, France (1040–1105), the greatest commentator of Bible and Talmud in Jewish tradition.

Reb Form of 'Rabbi', honorary title used in Eastern Europe, particularly for Chasidic teachers.

Satan Lit. 'adversary'. With time the term has come to denote a demoniac being who is the antagonist or rival of God but, almost invariably, is nevertheless under His control. He can oppose and obstruct the will of God, but never over-rule it.

Shabbat 'Sabbath', the seventh day in the creation story and the day of rest in Jewish tradition. Shabbat observance is central to the Jewish way of life.

Shechinah, Shekhinah Lit. 'indwelling'. Term for the Divine Presence with special reference to God's presence in the world.

Shulchan Aruch Lit. 'laid table'. The title of the most authoritative

Code of Law for Orthodox Jews, compiled by Joseph Karo (1488–1575).

Simchat Torah Lit. 'the rejoicing of the Torah'. The annual festival in the Jewish calendar when one cycle of the reading from the Pentateuch is concluded with the last section from *Deuteronomy* and the next cycle immediately commenced with the beginning of *Genesis*.

Talmud 'Learning'. After the conclusion of the Mishnah, schools in Babylonia and Palestine continued to discuss its content and harmonize it with other sources. The record of these discussions, together with the text of the Mishnah, is known as the Talmud. The Babylonian (and more authoritative) version was completed in the sixth century; the Palestinian some 150 years earlier.

Torah 'Instruction'. The Hebrew term for 'Pentateuch', primarily used to describe the whole body of Jewish tradition.

Yeshiva (pl. *yeshivot*) 'Seat' (of learning). The academies where Rabbinic literature is studied.

Yishuv Lit 'settlement', referring to the Jewish population of Palestine before the establishment of the State of Israel.

Yom Kippur 'Day of Atonement', the most important day in the Jewish calender.

Index

Abraham 58–9
Achad Ha-am 120
affirmation of God 176–8, 181, 189, 207
alienation 45–6, 175
Alves, R. A. 1
angel, guardian, of Esau 2–11, 17, 34–8, 181–2, 189
antinomianism 67, 80
anti-Semitism 15, 33; as anti-Zionism 42: and assimilation 29–30; causes of 195–9; and chosenness 173–5; as Gentile problem 165; and insecurity 195–8; and Jewish identity 27–31, 34, 41–2; meaning of 75; and survival 25–31; *see also* Auschwitz; Hitler; Holocaust; Nazism
Arabs 63, 180–2, 192–5; *see also* wars
archaeology 17, 25
assimilation: and anti-Semitism 29–30; and education 125; and social status 5–6; as threat 33–41, 171; *see also* Diaspora
Auschwitz 15, 32; God in 84, 101, 103; as 'great trial' 200; meaningless work in 135–6; *see also* anti-Semitism; Hitler; Holocaust; Nazism
Austria 30

automation 138
avodah 136, 146, 208

ba'al teshuvah 13, 25, 208
Bancroft, A. 139
Barmitsvah 25–7, 34, 53, 126–7, 208
Bar-On, M. 75
Bar Yochai, S. Rabbi 130
Begin, M. 64
being versus having 123–9, 145, 197
Berger, P. L. 52, 112
Berkovits, E. 84, 98, 102
Bettelheim, B. 23, 126
birth: control 39, 46, 142; rate 39, 180
bittachon 191, 208
black people 48
bondage 136–7
Bonhoeffer, D. 52
Borowitz, E. B. 157, 164, 168–70
bourgeois, Jews as 146
boys *see* Barmitsvah; masculinity
Britain: birth rate in 39; Orthodoxy in 12, 46–7, 80; Reform in 205; secularism in 53, 55
Buber, M. and Chasidism 131; on love 121; on marriage 143; against Orthodoxy 16–17; on Prophets 82; on